Be *Happy* Attitudes

Robert Schuller

WORD PUBLISHING
Dallas • London • Vancouver • Melbourne

THE BE-HAPPY ATTITUDES:
Eight Positive Attitudes That Can Transform Your Life!

Unless otherwise indicated, Scripture quotations are from the Revised Standard Version of the Bible, copyright 1946, 1952, 1971 and 1973 by the Division of Christian Education of the National Council of the Churches of Christ in the U.S.A. However, some verses have been very slightly modified to conform to the author's understanding of the intent of the original. Scriptures marked KJV are from the King James Version of the Bible. The scripture on p. 175 has been slightly modified to conform to modern usage.

All possible effort has been made to ensure that the poems quoted in this book are not currently under copyright. If an oversight has been made, the publisher will gladly correct it in future editions.

A slight change in the Paul Lawrence Dunbar poem on pp. 78–79 has been made to avoid offending modern sensibilities.

Library of Congress Cataloging-in-Publication Data

Schuller, Robert Harold.
The be-happy attitudes.

 1. Beatitudes. 2. Happiness—Religious aspects—Christianity. 1. Title.
BT382.S37   1985   226'.9306   85-17811
ISBN 0-8499-1426-4

Printed in the United States of America

 7 8 9 9 0 RRD 6 5 4 3 2

*To the congregation of the Crystal Cathedral
and the millions of friends
in the Hour of Power television ministry—
the people with whom I've laughed,
cried, and dreamed.
Together we have walked the walk
from sorrow to joy, from despair to victory.
Together we have seen and lived the
truth of our Lord's beautiful Be-Happy Attitudes.*

Acknowledgments

I am indeed grateful to those friends and loved ones who have so graciously allowed me to share their stories in this book. They join with me in the hope and prayer that others will find the secret of the Be-Happy Attitudes. I also extend my gratitude to Sheila Schuller Coleman, the editor of my weekly Sunday messages, who collected and organized my thoughts and anecdotal material. Her help in compiling this manuscript was immeasurable. And to Betty Cornell—thank you for the diligent hours you gave in research and clerical assistance.

Contents

Introduction

Happiness! Elusive, isn't it?
How often have you thought:

   🙣 If only I had that car . . . then I'd be satisfied!

   🙣 If only I could find someone truly to love me . . . then I'd be happy!

   🙣 If only I wasn't under so much financial stress . . . then I'd be content!

   🙣 If only . . .

   🙣 If only . . .

The news I have for you today is: All the "If only's" in the world—*even if they all came true*—still could not guarantee your happiness!

As we all have discovered at one time or another, cars, houses, jewelry, and other material gains don't bring happiness for long. After the immediate rush of joy at receiving something we have longed for, we are hit with the unique problems that every gain brings.

I'll never forget the young man who longed for a Ferrari. He dreamed about it. He imagined himself behind the wheel. He could smell the soft, supple leather. He could feel the power of the engine as it hugged the road.

Then it happened. He got the promotion he wanted, and with the promotion came a good-sized raise. At last he knew he could fulfill his fantasy.

Shining black, the Ferrari gleamed and glistened as he drove it away from the showroom floor. His dream had come true. He was ecstatic!

The car was magnificent to drive, and the young man loved all the attention he received from envious young men and lovely ladies. But the payments were steep. The entire raise and more was going into this car. The girls that the car attracted expected him to take them to expensive restaurants. They expected expensive gifts. And parking attendants expected fat tips.

Then it came time to have the Ferrari serviced. Wow! He had no idea that a mere lube job would cost so much. He managed to pay, although the high charges left him in the hole financially.

But it was worth it! He had a Ferrari—his dream car!

The young man enjoyed washing and waxing the Ferrari, rubbing the wax and watching the sun glint off the mirrored

"Attitudes are more important than facts!"

—Karl Menninger

body. But after a few months he began to notice little nicks in the paint and scratches on the door.

He began to get tired of the attention and the demands that the car and its new friends made on him. In fact, he was beginning to wonder who the girls were going out with—him or his car!

That car—the young man's pride and joy, his source of happiness—was beginning to become a source of disappointment and depression, as well as a burden. This letdown was totally unexpected. He had thought he would be eternally happy once he had that car. But he wasn't.

Future shock overtook—and shook—him. Now he was haunted by the question: "Will I ever be happy? Will I ever be satisfied?"

Material gains will not bring happiness. People who search for happiness in terms of money, real estate, possessions, or investment portfolios are always in for a rude awakening. All the money in the world will not buy happiness.

I have known some *very wealthy* people, and they have just as many problems as you and I do. They are no happier than you or I. In fact, money frequently brings with it *more* problems and less happiness. Wealthy people are often lonely and suspicious of people's motives.

If wealth can't guarantee happiness, then how about fame?

I have known famous people and many of them live a life

of despair. I'm sure that you can think of several movie stars and performers whose names were household words, who had achieved the highest level of fame, but who were so unhappy that they ended it all through suicide. Where do you look to find happiness?

🍀 *Riches?* It will take more than money.

🍀 *Recognition?* Fame is fleeting!

🍀 *Relationships?* Even those who love you will sometimes let you down.

🍀 *Recreational drugs?* They create habits that spell nothing but trouble!

How, then, do you find happiness? Not in riches, recognition, relationships, or recreational drugs, but in *readjusted mental attitudes!* That's what this book is about—*the life-transforming power of a readjusted mental attitude!* The good news is: Bad news can turn into good news if you readjust your attitude toward the tough times.

In this book:

🍀 You'll meet people who did just that!

🍀 You'll be introduced to eight spiritual laws, taught and lived out by Christ, that will help you realign and readjust your attitude!

❧ You'll be inspired to make the commitment to react positively to negative times!

This book will absolutely change your life—if you can learn to live by the Be-Happy Attitudes.

The Be-Happy Attitudes—what are they? You've probably heard of them as the "Beatitudes," the eight positive attitudes that come from the eight opening lines of Jesus of Nazareth's famous "Sermon on the Mount":

❧ "Blessed are the poor in spirit, for theirs is the kingdom of heaven."

❧ "Blessed are those who mourn, for they shall be comforted."

❧ "Blessed are the meek, for they shall inherit the earth."

❧ "Blessed are those who hunger and thirst for righteousness, for they shall be satisfied."

❧ "Blessed are the merciful, for they shall obtain mercy."

❧ "Blessed are the pure in heart, for they shall see God."

❧ "Blessed are the peacemakers, for they shall be called children of God."

❧ "Blessed are those who are persecuted for righteousness' sake, for theirs is the kingdom of heaven."

Blessed literally means "happy." So, whether you are winning or losing, succeeding or failing, enthusiastic or
depressed, happy or suffering, you can be happy if you will
discover the eight positive attitudes given to us by Jesus in
the Beatitudes.

Architect Philip Johnson, who designed the Crystal
Cathedral, says the most important part of any structure is
the "Goesinto"—that part or place where a person "goes into"
the experience.

What the "Goesinto" is to a building . . .

What the overture is to a symphony . . .

What the first serve is to tennis . . .

What the main entrance is to a facility . . .

What the glorious christening is to a ship . . .

What the opening salvo is to an argument . . .

What the first impression is to a new relationship . . .

What the opening number is to a program . . .

That's what these eight classic sentences are to the
teachings of Jesus. Classic—they've passed the test of time.
For over two thousand years they have transformed the
minds, the moods, the manners of men and women.

What is their secret? Why have they proven unsurpassed
as successful therapy to depressed minds? Now we know!

spiritual motivation to alter a human being's attitude. What we really have here is a therapeutic exercise in replacing negative attitudes with positive attitudes! Yes, here—unsurpassed in helpful literature—are eight positive attitudes that will transform any life! Discover them! Apply them! Enjoy life with these "Be-Happy Attitudes."

"I NEED HELP— I CAN'T DO IT ALONE!"

Blessed are the poor in spirit, for theirs is the kingdom of heaven.

WHO'S HAPPY today? Everybody has so many problems!" she snapped.

I had watched the television reporter approach this woman on the streets of New York City. She was obviously over-rushed, over-tense. The interviewer had simply asked her if she was happy. Now all I could see on my screen was the miserable side shot of an ill-mannered, ill-tempered woman whose negative attitude rang in my ears.

I wanted to speak up: *"Wait a minute, whoever you*

are! Happiness is not a question of having or not having problems. Everyone has problems, and not everyone is unhappy!"

Happiness is not dependent on whether or not we have problems, any more than it is dependent on whether or not we have material wealth. There are people who are happy even though they have very little. There are also people who are unhappy, even though they have the wealth of kings.

I have visited in the home and the office of a man whose personal fortune is measured in the tens of millions of dollars. And yet this man has financial problems. He has cash-flow problems. His wealth is all tied up in investments. He earns an awesome salary, but most of his paycheck goes into the equally awesome mortgage payments.

"Oh," but you say, "I'd gladly trade his financial security for my financial insecurity."

To that I reply, *"Nobody* is financially secure. The more you have, the more you can lose."

So, where do we find this elusive attitude of happiness? Where do we find escape from the entrapping problems that rob us of our joy? Where do we find the healing of our wounded hearts?

This question is all important, for too often, too many of us go to the wrong source for help.

I love the story of the man who went to his doctor. The doctor told him, "I'm sure I have the answer to your problem."

The man answered, "I certainly hope so, doctor. I should have come to you long ago."

The doctor asked, "Where did you go before?"

"I went to the pharmacist."

The doctor snidely remarked, "What kind of foolish advice did he give you?"

"He told me to come see you!"

We do go to the wrong places too often. If you have a medical problem, see your physician. If your problem is an unhappy spirit, then I have a spiritual doctor that I recommend. His name is Jesus Christ. Believe me, Jesus Christ was a joy-filled person. He had problems, but He knew how to handle them creatively and constructively.

Follow me through the next eight chapters. As we look upon the Beatitudes—the Be-Happy Attitudes—of Jesus Christ, you will discover our Lord's key to joyful living.

Joyous living is a grand possibility! Yes, even if we have problems! Financial problems? Wait a minute! Our reaction to our financial condition is far more important than the *reality* of the financial position.

After all, poverty is not just a matter of finances! Every one of us faces some kind of poverty; we all have a need at some level of our lives. It may be *financial* poverty. But it may also be *occupational* poverty, either a lack of success in our chosen profession or merely a lack of direction, lack of a dream or a goal. It may be *intellectual* poverty or *emotional* poverty.

3

Jesus begins the Beatitudes with a tremendous principle that has to do with this question of poverty: *"Blessed are the poor in spirit, for theirs is the kingdom of heaven."* The secret of successful living is simple: You and I must discover our soft spot, our weak link, our ignorant area, our poverty pocket. And then we must become "poor in spirit" as well—face up to our poverty, humble our attitude, acknowledge our weakness, ask for help.

OCCUPATIONAL POVERTY

Everybody is poor in his or her own way. Yours may be occupational poverty. If you are just starting out in life, you probably lack a dream. You need to know how to find a professional dream and how to pursue it. If you already have a goal toward which you're striving, you may lack an emotional support system which will carry you toward success.

If you are very successful, if you think you have arrived and you've got it made, you may also have a need. What is it? You may need to decide where you go from here and how you handle the success you have achieved.

If occupational success is eluding you, then the first Be-Happy Attitude verse is for you, for happiness will come when you surrender your arrogance and ask for help. Pride keeps us from crying out; greed also stops us. We want to take all the credit for our success. Let me share with you a valuable sentence I committed to memory long ago: "God

4

can do tremendous things through the person who doesn't care who gets the credit."

If you are willing to accept this basic premise, then you are willing to hire highly qualified people in your company or your corporation. They will make your business venture a success. They may get the credit, but you will be a success—and you will have helped not only yourself, but also everyone else around you.

Poverty handled in a pleasant, positive manner is an opportunity to involve good and generous people in our dreams, for often the strong welcome an opportunity to help the weak. The wealthy find meaning in their lives when they are given an opportunity to share in some worthy project or person. Today I enjoy the friendship of many wonderful people whom I met when I had to beg for their help to build a Crystal Cathedral or to spread a ministry via television.

I have been blessed because I have been poor—poor enough to swallow my pride and humbly ask for assistance. The result? Not merely success in reaching my occupational goals, but lasting friendships with those who saved the day for me.

So, don't become defensive about your lack by trying to gloss over it or pretending the problem doesn't exist. Chances are that such an attitude will end in futility and you'll end up paying an awful price. The way to handle your area of poverty is to say, "I need help."

INTELLECTUAL POVERTY

When I attended Hope College in Holland, Michigan, I studied economics under Dr. Edward Dimnent. It was said that Dr. Dimnent was so bright and so knowledgeable that he was qualified to teach any undergraduate course in the catalog of Hope College. He could handle biology, chemistry, physics—any course in the sciences— as well as the arts or humanities.

To top it all off, he was the architect of the college chapel! Such expertise was feasible forty years ago. Today it's impossible. The simple reason is that the accumulated knowledge in this world is more than one mind can comprehend. In addition, the rapid rate at which knowledge continues to be acquired through research precludes the possibility of anybody's ever reaching a point at which he or she can learn it all.

As a result, you might expect intellectual people to be more humble today than they were twenty or thirty years ago. It would seem logical that such an accumulation of knowledge would mean the end of intellectual elitism and academic arrogance. I'm not sure if that's happening. But the point is: Everybody is ignorant about something. *Every person has his area of intellectual poverty.*

Let me share with you a personal illustration. I attended a tiny country high school in Iowa which did not offer geometry. When I started my undergraduate studies at Hope

*You'll never
be licked
as long as
you know
what it is
you've lacked.*

College, Michigan, I discovered that everyone was required to take eight hours of science and that math courses were applicable to that requirement.

Consequently, I found myself in a math course. The first week the professor rattled off some statements which referred to geometric principles. Because I had never studied geometry, I didn't know what he was talking about. I noticed that the other students were nodding as if they completely understood, so I did as they did, thinking, "I'll pick it up later." The next week was the same. I didn't have the foggiest notion what the teacher was talking about, although I pretended I understood as clearly as my fellow students did. But the truth of the matter showed on my first test. I didn't get a good grade.

My professor approached me and kindly asked, "Are you having problems, Bob?"

I said, "Oh, no, I'm doing fine."

That was a lie. If I had been honest, I would have admitted that I had an enormous gap and lack from my pre-college work. But I didn't want to admit this fact because I didn't want the teacher to know how dumb I was. That was one of the biggest mistakes I ever made. *Poverty? Can it be a positive possibility?* Yes, if it motivates me to a humble cry for help. Had I reacted honestly, openly, and admitted my impoverishment to my professor, I now believe he would have knocked himself out tutoring and helping me! After all, the deepest need of the human being is the need to be needed. An admission of my poverty could have turned into a positive possibility for real learning. I could have pulled an A instead of a D if I had learned this lesson: Success starts when I dare to admit I need help!

I've seen businesses restored, students graduated, and marriages healed through this humble and hopeful attitude. And I've even seen it help in parent–teen relationships.

John was sixteen years old. He resented the way his father and mother treated him and talked down to him. What could he do? He could split and run away from home but things weren't that bad. So he pretended to ignore the problem by clamming up and refusing to discuss it.

John began to withdraw more and more into silence, sulking, and pouting. Then his parents became angry. "Why don't you say something?" was their frustrated attempt to converse with John. But his only reply was a shrug of his shoulders.

"Something wrong?" his parents would ask.

John would mumble, "No."

"Did we do something?"

"No."

"Why don't you say something?"

"What do you want me to say?"

Their relationship was at a stalemate until John took this Beatitude seriously and realized it was much smarter to say, "Mom, Dad, I have a problem with the way you treat me." It was the beginning of an open and honest relationship with his parents.

*What is
this pain?
It is the birth
pang of a new
attitude trying
to be born!*

Of course, parents also need this Beatitude. I would advise parents not to be afraid to be transparent with their children. Show them your weaknesses. Don't give them the impression you're perfect. Don't create shoes so large that your child will never be able to fill them. Be open, too. Share with them the predicament you find yourself in as a parent. Ask your teenager, "How would you handle this problem if you were the father or the mother?"

EMOTIONAL POVERTY

Cherry Boone O'Neill, the daughter of my friend, Pat Boone, tells of her struggle against the disease, anorexia nervosa, in her book, *Starving for Attention.** When she learned to face up to her emotional poverty and to love and accept herself at the deepest level, Cherry was able to overcome a shocking disease more widespread than anyone could dream.

Anorexia, also known as the "self-starver's disease," is a psychosomatic disorder that really begins on the emotional and psychological level and works its way outward to the physical level. By the time it manifests itself physically, professional help is needed, because the external manifestation—severe weight loss—is just a symptom of what's really happening inside.

Cherry says, "I got down to eighty pounds. I was wasting away. I really was on a slow suicide trip, because I hated myself

*New York: Continuum Publishing Co., 1982.

so badly. I didn't feel that God could possibly love me, considering what I was doing to myself and to the people that I loved. There was only a faint hope that God did exist and that there must be some way out of my mess. There were times when I prayed to die, because I didn't feel that I could come out of it.

"But my parents stuck by me, as did my husband, who literally went through thick and thin with me. Finally, we received some professional psychotherapy from a Christian psychiatrist. My husband and I moved up to the Seattle area, and through the course of six months of intensive therapy, I became better.

"I believe, without a shadow of a doubt, that God led me to the right doctor at the right time. For within six months I had changed from wanting to die to wanting to live, and I had learned that there were things about me that were worth loving in spite of what I did and what I looked like.

"The Lord has blessed me so much. He brought me through something as traumatic and horrendous as anorexia. He has given me a beautiful little girl, and now that I am on the other side I can give hope to other people who are going through it. There are almost one million people in the United States who have anorexia. And these people, as well as obese people, share a common problem, for all eating disorders have very similar roots. A lot of it has to do with that low self-esteem."

"Blessed are the poor in spirit…." So, blessed is Cherry Boone O'Neill. She dared to admit that she lacked self-esteem, she lacked the ability to lick the problem without help. So, today, she is happy with her family, her life, and—most of all—with herself.

Blessed are you when you face up to your emotional lack, admit your weakness. Blessed are you when you don't try to be an island and do it all by yourself.

ADMIT YOUR NEED—IT'S NOT EASY, BUT IT *IS* ESSENTIAL!

In all areas of our lives, the principle is the same: *Happiness comes when you admit where you are lacking and where you have a need.*

I remember years ago, when E. Stanley Jones used to conduct "ashrams" as he called them. An ashram is a term from India. It means a time of spiritual growth and expansion. Dr. Jones always began his ashrams by passing out pieces of paper and saying, "No one will see what you are about to write on this paper. I want you to write what your need is today."

It happened at every ashram. While people were thinking and praying and writing, someone would say, "Brother Stanley, I don't have a need. What do you write down if you don't have a need?" And Brother Stanley would say, "If you think you don't have a need, then *that's* your need!"

If it is true that each of us is poor somewhere in our lives, then why are we so reluctant to admit it? Consciously, or sometimes subconsciously, we develop defense mechanisms against exposure. We try to shield our-selves—especially in areas where we're vulnerable.

We are reluctant to admit our needs because we're afraid that people might really reject us. We're afraid of public embarrassment. Actually the problem is even deeper than that; it's a fundamental lack of self-esteem. We fear the lack of dignity that may come with rejection or embarrassment.

What we need to realize is that we don't need to be afraid of embarrassment or rejection. *What we do need to fear is the result that comes from hiding our lack, our need, our poverty.*

You may remember a time several years ago when the popular singer Tony Orlando announced "I quit!" in the mid-dle of a performance and left the stage—to the surprise of the audience, the press, even his associates, the singing group "Dawn."

Not long after that, our paths crossed, and Tony shared with me what happened that night:

"When I broke on that stage—and that's exactly what happened—I just simply could not stand physically anymore. I was saying things that didn't compliment my family. They didn't compliment my grandmother, who raised me, along with my mother, who so desperately tried to raise me with depth and character.

"Then I felt a silence. And this silence was so loud that it was godly. That silence was, in my opinion, conscience. And that conscience was the voice of the Lord that said,

'Tony, you must take care of yourself.' In my own heart I was saying, 'I've got to recuperate. I've got to reconstruct.'

"So I said to everyone, '*I quit!*' Actually, without realizing it, I really meant, '*I've got to begin again.*'

"The media, of course, dramatized my leaving the stage and embellished my words to make it sound as though I was saying, 'I quit show business.'

"In retrospect, however, I can honestly say I didn't really quit. I just stopped for a moment."

Then Tony referred to the Possibility Thinker's Creed:

> *When faced with a mountain,*
> *I will not quit!*
> *I will keep on striving*
> *until I climb over,*
> *find a pass through,*
> *tunnel underneath,*
> *or simply stay and turn*
> *the mountain into a gold mine—*
> *with God's help!*

He said, "I quit when Christ wasn't in my life. But I came back to this glorious life and this glorious business with the attitude that there is no way I can quit when I say, 'I am sorry for having offended You, O Lord. But I wasn't a friend of Yours then and didn't know You loved me as much as You do. I was wrong. Never again will I quit. I will keep on

15

If you're
too proud
(or too afraid)
to admit
you are hurting . . .

Don't be surprised
if nobody seems
to care.

striving until I find a pass through, tunnel underneath, or simply stay and turn that mountain into a gold mine.'

"To this day, I believe my career is more of a gold mine now than ever before."

THE BEGINNING OF A NEW BEGINNING

"Blessed are the poor in spirit...." How can this Be-Happy Attitude change you and me? By inspiring us to learn the power of two miracle-working confessions: (1) "I need help!" and (2) "I am sorry!"

"I Need Help!"

- "I've got a problem—can you help me?"

- "I don't understand—can you enlighten me?"

- "I can't agree with you—can we meet somewhere in the middle?"

- "I've got a problem accepting this—can you give a little from your position?"

- "I'm really at a loss—can you direct me?"

- "I'm ready to quit—what is your advice?"

- "I'm at my wits' end! I've had it!—Please tell me what you think I should do."

These forthright confessions are the beginning of a new beginning! Let's examine the miracle power available to us when we learn to say, "I need help."

If you feel trapped, lost, out-of-control, chained by difficulties, then I have good news for you. Your chains can lead to a change if you are willing to say these three words.

"Blessed are the poor in spirit." Happy is the one who knows where he or she is poor and is very open about it. Success comes to the person who is able to ask for help. The surprising thing is that admitting your need for help doesn't give your ego a blowout. On the contrary, it causes you to be a person of such emotional and intellectual integrity that people will trust you. And they will go along with you. In the process you will gain tremendous self-esteem.

The alternative is to play games, put on a front, pretend to be something you're not, and hope that no one will ever catch you without your mask on, your hair fixed just right, your guard up. You're not going to get the help you need by putting on a false front, by pretending you don't have a problem, or by hoping it will go away.

The truth is that there is somebody right now who would find great joy in helping you with your lack if he or she only knew that you had it. But if you pretend that you've got it made, with no problems, there's no way that person can help you.

There's always somebody ready to help anybody. Alcoholics Anonymous has been teaching this for years. A person will only find healing when he or she finally dares to admit, "Hey, I'm poor, I've got a problem. I'm helpless." When we get to this point, then we are ready to let go and let God take over.

A prominent personality who overcame alcoholism after a long struggle is a poignant illustration. In her words: "I struggled with my drinking problem for years. I kept saying, 'I can handle my liquor.' I refused to accept the truth that I was an alcoholic. I procrastinated; I rationalized: 'Some day I will cut down. I can handle it.' It was not until I hit the bottom that I was able to admit defeat and then say the three hardest words I ever uttered in my entire life: 'I need help!'"

It really works. I speak from experience. I was raised in an Iowa family where we always had bread with lots of butter. There was always an abundance of pie and other desserts. Consequently, I was a fat butterball when I was a baby, and I had to struggle with a weight problem as I grew up. I tried diets. I counted calories. (I still do.) But the weight accumulated through the years. Finally I decided that I would eat only lean meats, vegetables, and fresh fruits for dessert.

Then one night, almost seven years ago, I was taken out to dinner. The bread was passed. My host said, "This is fantastic. Feel it." I felt it; it was soft and warm. The fellow next to me was already spreading the butter, which was melting into the warm, fragrant bread. My host continued to tempt me. He said, "You must try the steak with the Bearnaise sauce." I followed his advice. By the time it came to dessert, I was feeling a little guilty. I was coaxed again, this time with, "They make the best pie here; it has a chocolate crust. You can't pass it by. Go on a diet tomorrow." I took the pie.

When I walked out of there, I calculated that I'd had about three thousand calories. That night I went to bed greatly depressed and filled with remorse. I woke up at two or three in the morning. I was racked with guilt. There was a total sense of futility because, frankly, it was the one area in which possibility thinking totally failed me. I could build churches, towers—even a cathedral. I could write books, but I could not get rid of my fat. I could raise millions of dollars to do God's work, but I couldn't turn my back on a piece of chocolate pie.

Now, in this black of my night, I prayed one simple prayer: "Dear Jesus, I don't know if You're dead or alive. I don't know if You are even real! I have believed it! I preached it! But I can't prove it by my weight control. Jesus, if You are there, can You help me?"

Poor in spirit, I admitted my lack. And instantaneously, an image went through my mind. I saw the old Floyd River on our family farm in Iowa. It was flooded way up to the grassy slopes. There in the middle of the stream was a great, gallant, strong tree that had been uprooted. It was being carried away by the current. Somehow I knew my body was that tree.

*If your
life is
really in a
mess . . . remember
this . . . stress
can be the start
of real success!*

The sloping hillside where the water lapped appeared very gentle. It didn't look wild; it didn't look rough. It seemed safe. But if I got too close to the water, the river could carry me away. That was what butter, ice cream, and cake were for me. I'd take one bite, thinking I could stop after one simple little taste. But one bite always led to another . . . and another . . . and another. I was being destroyed by a seemingly harmless little bite. Then I heard the message. It was in the past perfect tense: "I have snatched you from destruction."

I had to refrain from tasting, from the nibbles that led to whole meals. I had an internal transformation. I knew then that I had been liberated from subconscious forces that kept me addicted to sweets. I still have my little ups and downs, but never have I reverted to what I was.

The Lord helped me once I admitted that I was unable to do it without Him. As long as I continued to believe that I could safely eat a little here and there and remain in control, I was doomed. But when I cried out for help, I was saved! "Blessed are the poor in spirit, for theirs is the kingdom of heaven."

"I'm Sorry!"

When you learn to make this confession, you'll find happiness, because you will discover the miracle-working power to be an honest person. You and I are free when we admit we've been wrong. Instead of an ego trip, we are on an integrity trip—the road to real happiness. For the integrity trip really feeds our self-esteem. We can be proud of ourselves for being open and honest and humble! By contrast, the ego trip is a constant threat and finally fatal to genuine self-respect!

On the integrity trip we're no longer slaves to perfectionism. So we aren't embarrassed when people catch us making mistakes. When we have done something wrong, we need only say, "I'm sorry." To the ones we've hurt we can say, "I'm a human being. The Lord has forgiven me. I've forgiven myself; I hope you will too."

I will never forget the morning I asked my oldest daughter, Sheila, to do the breakfast dishes before school. Not realizing that she was already running late and facing too many tardy notices, I was stunned by her reaction. She burst into profuse tears.

Again, misinterpreting the motive behind the outburst, assuming that she was merely trying to get out of an unpleasant chore, I demanded that she dry her eyes and get to work—*immediately.*

She reluctantly obeyed me, but I could hear her anger in the careless clanking of the dishes in the sink. On the way to school, she turned her back to me and stared sullenly out the window.

Usually, I took positive advantage of the uninterrupted time that I was able to spend with my children while driving them to school by teaching them poetry or Bible verses or just sharing together.

On that morning, however, there were no poems, no verses, no songs—only deathly, stubborn silence. I dropped Sheila off, mumbled a good-bye and left for my office. I tried to work, but I couldn't concentrate. All I could see was the scared, tear-stained face of my daughter as she hesitantly climbed out of the car to face her teacher and classmates.

I had begun to realize that my timing had been way off. I had no right to demand that she do the dishes without giving her some forewarning, some planning time. I realized that I had been wrong to upset her so close to the time when she was going to be facing peers, a time when she needed support.

The more I thought about it, the more remorseful I became. Finally, I decided that I had to do something. I had to say I was sorry, and my apology could not wait until suppertime. So, I called the school and I asked the counselor for permission to take her to lunch.

I shall never forget the look of surprise on her face when she saw me waiting for her in the office. I said, "Sheila, I've gotten permission to take you to lunch. They said that you could have an hour off. Let's go."

I led her by the arm down the empty school corridor. As soon as the heavy doors slammed behind us, I turned to my daughter and I said, "Sheila, I'm sorry. I'm so very sorry! It's not that I shouldn't have asked you to help out at home, but I had no right to insist on it this morning without any previous warning. I upset you at a time when you most needed my love and support—just before you went to school. And I let you go without saying 'I love you.' I was wrong. Please forgive me."

Sheila put her arms around my neck and hugged me and said, "Oh, Dad, of course I forgive you. I love you, too."

Oh, the power of those restorative words, "I'm sorry!" They heal relationships—between ourselves and our friends and loved ones, and between ourselves and our Lord.

The psalmist wrote, "A broken and contrite heart, O God, thou wilt not despise" (Ps. 51:17).

He wrote for many. Throughout the Scriptures we see them—the broken and contrite:

- The penitent thief

- The prodigal son

- David, the adulterer

- Saul of Tarsus, a murderer of Christians

- Mary Magdalene, the prostitute

These scalawags—what do they all have in common? They all belong to God's Hall of Fame. In the corridors of heaven they all have positions of honor.

How did they acquire such noble recognition? All of them reached a point in their personal shortcomings, sin, and shame when they cried out, "O God, be merciful to me, a sinner!"

Yes, if your life is in a mess, stress can lead to real success—for after all, *real* success is being admitted to the Kingdom of heaven.

You and I need this humble attitude, to be poor in spirit, in our spiritual lives. You and I need it in our prayer lives. What if you have doubts? What do you do with them? Do you pretend they'll go away? Act as if they don't exist? Sing the songs, read the prayers? Act as if you really believe? No. Rather, go to God and say, "If you're there, God . . . to tell the truth, I don't even believe in You right now. I wish I could. If it's wrong to doubt, I hope you'll forgive me!"

Once you start being honest, in all of life and especially in your prayers, it's amazing what will break loose for you. Don't try kidding anybody, least of all yourself.

"Blessed are the poor in spirit, for theirs is the kingdom of heaven." If you have a need, God has an answer. He specializes in matching up answers to problems, healings to hurts, and solutions to perplexing situations.

WHAT'S HOLDING YOU BACK?

Only when you and I reach those depths of despair are we then on the way to joy, because God particularly pours out His blessings upon those who know how much they need Him. The *promise* is joy. The *principle* is to ask God for help,

*It takes
guts . . .
to leave
the ruts!*

admit we cannot do it alone. The *problem,* of course, that stands in the way of our crying out to God is the problem of an *unholy pride*.

There is such a thing as a holy pride—self-esteem and self-respect represent a healthy pride in ourselves as God's loved and redeemed creation. But arrogance and vanity result from an unholy pride that says, "Get out of my way, I want to do it myself"—like a stubborn small child refusing a loving parent's help.

"Blessed are the poor in spirit, for theirs is the kingdom of heaven." And so you and I come to a time when we stop playing games and putting on false fronts. We reach a point in life when we know that we are spiritually bankrupt. It is at this point that we kneel before our Lord and say, "God, I want to be born again. I want a new life. I want a joyful Christ to come and live in me. Oh God, I turn my life over to You."

A few years ago I received a letter that touched me deeply. Its impact had as much to do with who the writer was—her credentials and her professional integrity—as it had to do with *what* she said.

The letter was from Dr. Mary Ellen Bening, who works at the United States International University in San Diego. She has her Ph.D. in Social Sciences. Her job is to edit doctoral dissertations that are being produced at the university. This impressed me because it meant she would naturally be very up-to-date as to the latest research in human behavior.

Dear Dr. Schuller:

On the 26th of August my husband and I attended the 11:15 service at your son's church to hear your sermon. I shook your hand after the service but was unable to speak to you. What I had experienced during the service left me speechless.

My reason for coming that Sunday was that two weeks earlier I had listened for the first time to a televised service from the Crystal Cathedral. On other occasions when services were being aired I had turned to other channels in search of nonreligious programs; however, your sermon on life's contradictions captured my attention. . . . [In your sermon] you demonstrated that it is not a contradiction to be a deeply reflective, reasoning human being and an adamantly faithful Christian. . . . After hearing your sermon I could not stop thinking about its meanings and diverse applications. I also began to think about the alternative path which Christ offered, and for the first time I began not only to see but to feel the precious gift He gives. When I awakened on the 26th, I had the feeling that perhaps I was ready to receive that gift.

Your sermon that morning, entitled "Breaking Through: There's Hope for You," focused on faith, a capacity I most needed to understand, because my earlier inability to grasp the meaning of faith had prevented me from becoming a Christian. I had imagined that certain fortunate people experienced a calling from God, were mystically touched, felt a spiritual awakening, and hence received the faith. It never occurred to me that faith is an option!

My husband and I arrived early at the church on that special Sunday. And as the service began something wonderful happened. I felt myself being enveloped in peace, love, and strength. I would call it a spiritual renaissance except that I cannot remember feeling so alive before. I experienced a birth in the church that day, and I was amazed at how simple it really was! I had assumed that I would have to pass some monumental test before I would be qualified to take my rightful place in a church. Faith seemed like another degree, the most advanced of degrees, that one earns after unlocking the secrets of the universe.

In reality, God asked so little and gave in return so much!

Mary Ellen Bening

Here was a letter from an intellectual—a very learned, bright young woman. She had thought she had it altogether, never dreaming that she lacked anything or needed anything beyond her ability to think and learn and perceive. And yet, even Dr. Bening had been lacking. Spiritually she had been empty; spiritually she had been impoverished. Her soul had been dry and thirsty and craving for something—what it was, she hadn't known.

But then she saw her lack. She saw what it was she needed. She needed to believe in the loving, saving grace of Jesus Christ.

She became poor in spirit when she realized that in the process she didn't have to become poor in intellect. When she saw that she could be a believer in Jesus without sacrificing her intellectual integrity, she grappled Jesus to her side, embraced Him with her soul, and was born again.

When you discover the secret of the first Be-Happy Attitude, when you are able to say "I need help!" or "I'm sorry!" or "I have a lack!", then you will have taken the important first step toward being truly happy. For then you will have the attitude that can free you to move into the other Be-Happy Attitudes.

I strongly believe that there is a logical progression to the Beatitudes. Jesus gave them to us in the order He did for a very important reason: They are interdependent on each other, and one is a prerequisite for the next. Think about it. Before Jesus can comfort us, before He can help us and heal us, we must have the attitude that we are *willing* to be helped! He cannot make us happy unless we *want* to be happy.

So are you willing to be helped? Do you want to be happy? Are there some areas in your life where you are lacking and need some help? Then Be-Happy. For you have the one essential ingredient you need to begin discovering the secret of the remaining Be-Happy Attitudes.

"I'M REALLY HURTING— BUT I'M GOING TO BOUNCE BACK!"

Blessed are those who mourn, for they shall be comforted.

R. SCHULLER, *why do bad things happen to good people?"* I can't tell you how often I've faced this question in the forty-five years I have spent as a pastor.

I answer, "Part of the problem is that we ask the wrong questions. If we ask the wrong questions we're never going to come up with the right answers."

"Why do bad things happen to good people?" This is the

wrong question, because it's the one question God never answers.

The Old Testament prophets lamented in times of trouble, *"Why, O Lord?"* Always He remained silent to that question. Even when Jesus Himself cried out from the cross, "My God, my God, *why?"* God didn't answer.

God never answers the *why,* because the person who asks "why" doesn't really want an explanation; he wants an argument! God refuses to be drawn into an argument. If God answered one "why," we would come with another. There would be no end to it.

If the wrong question is *"Why do bad things happen to good people?"* then what is the right question? It is *"What happens to good people when bad things happen to them?"*

Jesus answered that question in the Beatitudes. In the second Beatitude, which is the subject of this chapter, the reality of tough situations is confronted head-on. Jesus says, in essence, "When bad things happen to good people, they are blessed, for they are comforted."

Christianity isn't a Pollyanna religion. It doesn't claim that bad things won't happen to us. We are never told in the Old or New Testament that if we live a good life we'll never have any sickness or tragedy. However, we are promised in Isaiah 43: "Fear not, for I have redeemed you; I have called you by name, you are mine. When you pass through the waters . . . they shall not overwhelm you; when you walk through fire you shall not be burned, and the

34

flame shall not consume you. For I am the Lord your God"(vv.1–3).

If God keeps His promises, then how does He comfort good people when bad things happen to them?

As a pastor, I am in the specialized work of dealing with the hurt, the lonely, the suffering, the sick, the dying. For thirty-five years I have been trudging the soft green lawns of cemeteries with my arms around young wives, husbands, fathers, mothers, relatives, and other loved ones. I have watched caskets lowered—hundreds of them: tiny ones, medium sized and large ones—draped in flowers and flags. I have seen people buried in graduation gowns, pulpit gowns, bridal dresses. Believe me, I am not blind to the reality of suffering. I have walked and wept my way through much human sorrow.

NO TWO SORROWS ARE THE SAME

A vast number and variety of human emotional experiences come under the general label "sorrow." Marie, a friend of mine and a member of my congregation, shared these intimate feelings with me upon the death of her husband: "No two sorrows are the same. I lost my son as a teenager; I lost my daughter in her twenties. Now my husband has passed away. Each grief has been painful, but each grief has been different."

Over and over I've seen sorrow, and over and over again

35

I have witnessed this one fact: *God does comfort good people when bad things happen to them.* It is possible to be happy even in a world where sorrow casts its long, gray shadow.

Trouble never leaves us where it finds us; sorrow will change our tomorrow. But God inspires us to become better people, not bitter ones. He shows us the negative can be turned into a positive, a minus into a plus, and that's what the cross is all about.

How can we find relief from grief? How can we turn our mourning into a morning? (1) Realize what you can do for yourself! (2) Realize what God can do for you!

HERE'S WHAT YOU CAN DO!

Don't Blame God!

If you are going through a heartbreak and really having a difficult time, don't blame God! Human error is always the culprit: error of judgment, error of will, or error of purpose. Human selfishness, indifference, rebellion, folly, stupidity, brashness can always be found as the root cause of human misery and suffering.

Cancer and heart disease, along with other related illnesses, are the top killers in America today. No one will ever be able to place the blame for these diseases on God. In time, or in eternity, we shall see the truth: all disease is dis-ease, a lack of harmony between a human organism and its environment. Disease is too often caused by not eating right, not sleeping right, not exercising right, not breathing or breeding right; it is a question of man's not attaining a harmonious balance with his surroundings. If disease appears, man is doing something wrong; God is not to blame!

But, you say, can't we blame God for not showing us how certain deaths could be avoided or how certain illnesses could have been cured?

Think a moment. The real problem is not our ignorance, but our carelessness. Almost all disease, death, and sorrow is brought upon us not through lack of knowledge, but through lack of obedience to the light God has given us through several different channels:

(1) *God revealed the Ten Commandments.* He gave us these ten laws to protect us from an alluring, tempting path which would ultimately lead only to sickness, sin, and sorrow. Following the Ten Commandments will result in spiritual health, mental health, and physical health! Killing, lying, stealing, and adultery are bad for the health! (Consider the current epidemic of venereal diseases!) Under the banner of sophistication and liberation, many of us tell God to go to hell! In so doing, we only send ourselves there.

(2) *God revealed secrets of health.* He has given us throughout the Bible, as well as through medical

37

science, guidelines for us to follow regarding our daily bodily habits of eating, drinking, sleeping, working, exercising. Yet, it is true: Some doctors still smoke and drink to excess. Some ministers eat improperly. Some athletes fail to exercise often enough, and generally overlook their physical well-being. Can we honestly and fairly accuse God for not giving us more insight into health when we blatantly disregard the knowledge He *has* revealed?

(3) *God disclosed secrets of salvation from sin.* We know that sorrow, separation, sickness, and disease are ultimately caused by sin. We know that much physical illness is caused by mental tension, stress, worry, anxiety, fear, and guilt. We also know that if we accept salvation and yield our minds and our hearts to the saving Spirit of Christ, our negative sins and emotions will be drawn out and healing of mind and body will begin. Yet, many of us are still hesitant to give ourselves over completely to Christ. We reject God's salvation.

Can we not then blame God for permitting people to be so selfish? Doesn't God have the power to control every person on earth, to force everyone to obey Him? Should we not blame God for creating man with the capacity to sin?

Consider for a minute the dilemmas that God faced at the dawn of creation. When God created humankind, His

*What happens
to good people
when bad things
happen to them?*

*They become ...
better people*

objective was to make a material form of life which would be a reflection of His own nonmaterial Self. Thus, He chose to make man "after His image," a decision-making creature, capable of discernment, judgment, evaluation, choice, and decision.

When God created such a person, He realized fully that this creature would have the power to decide against God. But let's look at the alternative. If He had designed a man who could never make a wrong decision, this creature would never be able to make a personal decision of his own. He would be nothing but a perfect, sinless, guiltless, error-free . . . person? NO! Machine? Yes! Computer? Yes! Human being . . . NEVER! God decided to take the greatest gamble of the ages—to make an opinion-forming, idea-collecting, decision-making creature. What He created was a potential sinner, but a potentially loving person as well.

Don't blame God for permitting sin. Thank God that He has never, in spite of our sins, taken our freedom from us and with it our capability of becoming sincere, loving persons. Don't blame God for the suffering in this world! Blame human beings for personally choosing the path leading to heartache and sorrow. Blame human beings for rejecting the divine truth when it was shown to them. Blame human beings for refusing God's salvation, even when offered in the name of Jesus! You have but to look at the cross and know that no human being can ever blame God for not going to the limit to save us.

Don't Blame Yourself

Grief always seems to be associated with guilt. But self-condemnation will solve no problem and will change no circumstance. It is merely a negative, nonconstructive emotion which can wreak havoc in your life.

You probably remember reading about the tragic accident at the Hyatt Regency in Kansas City several years ago. If you recall, one hundred fourteen people were killed and many more injured when a concrete walkway encircling the atrium collapsed. A young friend of mine was there that night and witnessed the horror. As she said to me later, "Dr. Schuller, it was like being in a disaster movie. The only difference was that this was *real!* I wanted desperately for someone to take it back and fix it, put it back the way it was before."

Of course there was no way of undoing the damage. People all around my friend were dying. She wasn't trained in emergency procedures, so there was nothing that she could do. That feeling of helplessness, coupled with the horrific memories, nearly destroyed her.

She explained, "There was nothing I could do. I could get handkerchiefs all night, but it didn't bring people back. I went home that night and couldn't sleep. The guilt was overwhelming because I couldn't make them live. Hundreds were dying and there was nothing I could do.

"I've been a Christian all my life, so I prayed and prayed

41

that people would live. They published in the paper a list of the names of the victims that were still hospitalized. Daily, I prayed for them. But I just couldn't seem to overcome the guilt that came with my sense of helplessness. So, I started to withdraw. I withdrew from friends that I'd made before, and I didn't try to make new ones. People who know me will tell you that such behavior is really against my character. I held everything inside. I wouldn't talk to anybody about it. I guess you could say that I just stopped living.

"I felt that I should have died in the disaster. Why was I alive when so many others were dead? No one can understand unless they have been through a disaster. No one can know how deep that hurt is. I just didn't want to hurt anymore. I determined to end my life. I intended to overdose on drugs. So, I arranged for one of my girlfriends to pick my children up, and I started taking the drug my doctor had prescribed for depression. I was about halfway through the bottle when I thought about how much I loved my family and how much my family loved me. I called the telephone hotline you have here at the Crystal Cathedral—NEW HOPE.

"The counselor at NEW HOPE asked me questions about myself. He said, 'It sounds like you've got a lot to live for.' He kept telling me that I had a lot of things I still needed to do and a lot of people that I could still help. Somehow, he instilled something in me that no one else had been able to do.

"Meanwhile he had called the police. The paramedics

took me to the hospital, but by the time I arrived I was in a coma. I remained in a coma for three days. There was no brain activity whatsoever. I was pronounced clinically dead and my family was called to see me before they unplugged the life-support systems.

"People had been praying for me and one of my uncles whom I'd been very close to all my life was standing there holding my hand and telling me that he loved me. My subconscious heard him, I guess, for I opened my eyes about three hours before they were going to unplug the machine.

"Everything that has happened since has been better than I could ever have dreamed. I wish I could tell everyone who's depressed, or anyone who's thought about dying or killing themselves, that it passes! It may not seem like it, but it does pass and it always gets better."

DON'T FIX THE BLAME— FIX THE PROBLEM

A member of our church showed me a slogan used by the company where she works:

DON'T FIX THE BLAME, FIX THE PROBLEM!

What is your problem? First, recognize that the real problem is not the tragedy that has hit. The real problem is your reaction to it. If you do not take control of your reaction

*What is
the cross?
It is
a minus*

—

*turned
into a plus!*

†

to your loss, you can and probably will eventually be destroyed by it.

How do you "fix the problem"?

(1) *Decide not to go on for the rest of your life surrendering to sorrow and tears.* To do this only disgraces your loved ones, your friends, and yourself. Moreover, continued grief dishonors the God who wants only to be credited with giving you a rebirth of joy! Decide that this non-constructive sorrow mixed with self-pity has to STOP!

We can all take a lesson on handling our grief from Andre Thorton. Andre, a valuable hitter for the Cleveland Indians for nearly a decade, went through a tragedy that would have devastated most of us. In 1977, Andre, his wife, and their two children were driving to Pennsylvania to take part in her sister's wedding. In that part of the country, the weather can turn bad even as early as October. As they started their journey that evening, it began to rain. Then it snowed. As they wound their way through the mountains of Pennsylvania, the winds became very strong, caught the back end of their van, and caused it to spin and turn over. They hit a guard rail. Andre was knocked unconscious.

When he woke up, he was lying in a hospital bed next to his son. A short time after he regained consciousness, a nurse came over and said, "Andre, I'm sorry to have to tell you this." She began to cry. Then she said simply, "The coroner is with your wife and daughter."

Andre told me, "It was a gut-wrenching time. I felt as

though the insides of my body were being torn out. But even at that moment we can count on the Lord's Word. The Lord said in His Word, *'I will never fail you nor forsake you'* (Heb. 13:5).

"His Word was there. I'm so thankful that I was a Christian and had been for a number of years before that. So I was able to trust in that Word and to trust in my Lord at that particular time.

"I know that Christ was there with us in the midst of our most difficult moments. The Lord's strength upheld my son and me and allowed us to go on. I think the greatest thing I learned at that point is that our God is faithful."

I had to ask Andre, "But to lose your wife whom you loved and adored as well as your darling daughter—did you never doubt God's love?"

Andre's reply was wonderful. He said, "I think we all have periods when we wonder if we could have done something differently. I was no different from anyone else. But I'm thankful that God doesn't let us entertain those thoughts. Rather than entertaining those thoughts of doubt, I could trust God and know that whatever He was working out, whatever plan He had set down, was a plan that was going to glorify Him. When I look back at the tragedy today, I see the lives that were touched by what the Lord has done through our lives. And so I see no longer a tragedy, but a joy, as other lives are brought back out of a living death to abundant life!"

"You know, Andre," I said, "Psalm 23 says, 'Surely goodness and mercy shall follow me all the days of my life' [v. 6]. When you cannot see the goodness of God, you can experience His mercy. That's what you have experienced, Andre."

"Oh, there's no doubt about that!" he answered. "I am a child of God merely by the acceptance of His Son. As God's child, I know that He directs and guides my life. Proverbs 16:9 says, 'A man's heart chooses his way, but God directs his steps.' I chose the way of Christ as my Savior, and God directs my steps. I'm thankful for that because I don't have to wonder where I'm going."

"Where did you get this faith?" I asked.

"I grew up in a difficult time, when there was a lot of confusion in our country and a lot of questions on my mind. I saw my best friend stabbed to death at the age of seventeen. I grew up in the tremendous confusion of racial tension. The Vietnam War was at its height. People were saying God was dead. Naturally, it was a time when a young person like myself asked many questions. I was no different. I asked questions such as: 'Where are we going? What is life all about? Who's the justifier of life?'

"I can remember my mother saying to me, 'Andre, I can't answer all of those questions for you, but I can direct you to the One who can.'

"I was going away to Fort Dix, New Jersey, as part of the Pennsylvania National Guard. When I left, Mother gave me a Bible, and when I got to the barracks I began to read and study it. At that time I didn't believe there was no God; I just didn't know Him to the point where I could grab hold of Him and say, 'Father, help me!'

"After reading the Bible I realized that I was God's child, that the gap which separated me from Him had been bridged by the death and resurrection of His Son, Jesus. That joy and assurance was what I needed to see that there was a greater hope than what the world had to offer.

"So, you ask me where I got my faith? I'll tell you: I got it from my mother. I thank God that I had a mother who loved her son so much that she shared with him the most precious thing she could give him—the gift of her faith!"

Andre was not destroyed when he lost his wife and his daughter. God gave him the strength to go on with his life. Today Andre has married again and has a new baby. He carried on, he kept on going, and didn't stop living when his wife and daughter did!

(2) *Do* not *accept defeat.* Somehow we must learn to accept the reality of the bad things that happen to us without accepting emotional defeat. "The death thy death hath dealt to me is worse than the death thy death hath dealt to thee!" These words were spoken by a widow as she stood looking at the body of her dead husband. Do not quit! Tough times never last, but tough people do! Be brave! Fight back! Come back again. There is a world out there—hungry, hurting. Think of them—they are alive; they need you!

In the book *Gone with the Wind,* we read about the Southern gentleman who broke down under the tragedies involved in the Civil War. Observing his collapse, another character in the novel philosophizes, "He could be licked from the inside. I mean to say that what the world could not do, his own heart could." Then the simple philosopher concluded, "There ain't anything from the outside that can lick any of us."

(3) *Bury your selfish griefs.* Grief which keeps you from thinking of and helping others is selfish. Around you is a world filled with living human beings who are hurting more than you are. There are lonely, heartbroken, dying women . . . men . . . children out here! They need you. You are stronger than they are. You can comfort them. The secret of happiness that is reiterated throughout the Beatitudes can be summed up in two words: "I'm third." Are you hurting? How do you come back alive again? Think of God first, think of others second, and then put yourself third.

(4) *Add up your joys; never count your sorrows.* Look at what you have left in your life; never look at what you have lost. At a time of sorrow you are so overwhelmed and swamped by the shock, the pain, and the grief that you are not even conscious of the joys that still are alive deep under that blanket of grief. Determine to uncover your smothered joys and let them breathe and flourish again! There are many things that you are still thankful for, even though you do not feel your gratitude. Begin by reminiscing. Relive your happy memories. Treat yourself to replays of that great collection of joyful experiences that have occurred in your past. There are many wonderful things that have happened to you in life.

I have a friend who keeps an "Italian philosophy" poem on his restaurant wall. The following are the words, worth remembering:

> *Count your garden by the flowers,*
> *Never by the leaves that fall.*
> *Count your days by golden hours,*
> *Don't remember clouds at all.*
> *Count your nights by stars, not shadows,*
> *Count your life with smiles, not tears.*
> *And with joy on every birthday,*
> *Count your age by friends, not years.*

(5) *Turn your sorrow into a servant.* Once you have buried your griefs, you are ready to turn your sorrow into a helpful partner. Grief can be a demonic dictator if you let it. It can turn you into a cynical, doubting, resentful, self-pitying recluse or drunkard. Or it can be your servant, helping you to feel more compassion for others who hurt, giving you visions for new avenues for ministry. Make the positive choice—let your sorrow become a servant that will serve God and your fellow man!

I recently received a letter from a New York viewer of my television program. I have read and re-read the letter so often that I know it almost by memory. Let me share it with you:

Dear Dr. Schuller:

I have never written a letter like this before in my life. This is the story of a bitter man . . . and the person who saved him. I am that bitter man. In 1961 I was married. I love my wife. Our love is the only thing that has kept me going. Shortly after our marriage we suffered a financial reverse. This really made me bitter.

Then we wanted children and discovered we could have none. This made me more bitter. After a while we adopted a child and for a brief time, we were very happy. Then we discovered that this adopted child, a little boy we had named Joey, was mentally retarded because of brain damage! That made me more bitter. But the bitterest day in my life was the day that Little Joey died. When we buried him, I was so bitter, I didn't believe in God, Christ, or anybody or anything.

For some months now my wife has been watching this religious television program on Sunday mornings. She begged me to watch with her, but I wouldn't. Six weeks ago, I happened to walk through the living room, when something you said caught my attention. I listened. I also listened the next week, and the next, and the next. I am writing to tell you that in six short weeks I am

*The good
news is …
the bad news
can be turned into
good news …
when you
change your
attitude!*

now a changed person. All my bitterness is gone.

I am thanking you because you introduced me to *Jesus Christ*. Because of this, my wife and I have decided to dedicate our lives to helping mentally retarded children. I can't tell you what a changed life I have because my thinking has changed through Christ!

I am joyfully yours, an "Hour of Power" listener.

Let your sorrow turn you into a better person and your sorrow will turn out to be a blessing!

(6) *Accept the comfort that God is trying to offer you.* At the beginning of this chapter, I said that God is not the source of sorrow. Man's sin brought sorrow and continues to bring sorrow into this world. God moves in immediately and forthrightly to bring comfort. He offers the comfort of His promises of love and eternal life.

"Blessed are those who mourn, for they shall be comforted." Yes, there's a condition attached, an "if" connected. You will be blessed, you will be comforted, *if* God is your friend, and *if* Christ is your savior. Accept this comfort that God offers to you.

HERE'S WHAT GOD WILL DO!

God offers *real* comfort. Not neurotic pity. Not a sympathy that only weakens the hurting person. He offers a tough love that turns us into sweeter and stronger persons!

When our daughter Carol lost her leg in a motorcycle accident at the age of thirteen, my wife and I fell over ourselves trying to comfort her. We brought her favorite stuffed animals to the hospital, we called her friends and asked them to visit with her. We never left Carol's side; one of us was with her almost constantly.

Then one day we received a call from our friend, Dorothy DeBolt. As many of you know, Dorothy is the mother of fourteen adopted children. Those children are all very special. Some are blind, some are paraplegic. One is a quadruple amputee. All are physically or mentally challenged children.

Dorothy has done wonders with all of these children. Despite their handicaps, she has motivated them to do far more than anyone would ever have dreamed. They all dress themselves. There are no ramps in the house; they all know how to climb stairs so that they would never be barred anywhere by the absence of ramps.

When Dorothy heard about Carol's accident, she called to express her love and concern. Yes, she expressed love—she cared that Carol had experienced so much pain. And yes, she was concerned. She felt Arvella and I needed to be warned that there was a right way and a wrong way to help Carol.

She said simply, "Be careful how you comfort her."

How wise were her words. Carol needed comfort, not pity, and comfort came not by drying her tears, but by lifting her attention beyond the present pain to the future victories.

God comforts. He doesn't pity. He doesn't commiserate. He picks us up, dries our tears, soothes our fears, and lifts our thoughts beyond the hurt. How does God comfort us so masterfully? Five ways: (1) He gives us courage; (2) He gives us a sense of calm; (3) He gives us companionship; (4) He gives us compassion; and (5) He gives us a new set of commitments.

GOD GIVES US COURAGE

When we are in despair, God gives us the courage to go on, to live through our grief, to pick ourselves up to the point where we can face tomorrow. I'll never forget the time several years ago when I received a call from the family of Senator Hubert Humphrey, who by then was dying of cancer. His family asked me to visit them, hoping I could inspire him to go back to Washington, D.C., one more time. When I arrived at the little apartment in Minneapolis, he was waiting for me. He sat, gaunt, upright in a chair, completely dressed. His white shirt was about an inch and a half larger than his thin neck.

That was courage! It took a lot of courage to put on a shirt and tie—to put trousers on, shoes and socks, and to sit up in a chair. When you are that sick, that's a big step forward, believe it or not. Where does such courage to move ahead come from? It comes from God.

I said to this courageous man, "Hubert, when you have

been really down, depressed, and discouraged, what brought you back up again?" I hoped the question would cause him to recall times when he'd been victorious over depressing circumstances.

He began to recall some Bible verses, slogans, and inspiring experiences. Suddenly, I saw a spark in his eye! So I said to him, "When are you going back to Washington?"

He looked at his wife, Muriel, and said, "Maybe I should—once more."

He did—and lived his last weeks out as he lived his life—bravely. I was honored to preach the funeral sermon only a few months later, with Billy Graham, Jesse Jackson, President Carter, and nearly every ranking Senator in the congregation. I am told nearly forty million Americans listened and watched over the television networks.

I chose for that message the topic "Courage—The Big C." "'The Big C'—that's what they call cancer," I said. "Hubert Humphrey knew that, but he knew a bigger 'C'—Courage!"

GOD GIVES US A SENSE OF CALM

How does God comfort people when bad things happen to them? He gives them courage. He also gives them a sense of calm—in the most unexpected times and ways. As it is said in an old Christian hymn, "Sometimes the light surprises a Christian while he sings; it is the Lord who comes with healing on His wings."

I recall the sister of the late congressman Clyde Doyle. She had two children, a son and a daughter. Both of them were killed when they were teenagers. Her husband also died at a fairly early age. She was completely alone. You know, it's easy to go to someone and say, "Don't look at what you have lost, look at what you still have." But here was a woman who had no one left!

I asked, "Where did you find comfort? What gives you the strength to keep going?"

She said, "I live in Long Beach. I used to go to the beach every day. Often I just sat there numb. I could not think, I could not feel, but I could still see. And I watched the waves as they built into a curl of foam, as they washed up onto the sand and then retreated. I did that day after day, week after week, month after month, and year after year. One day, as I watched the wave curl, break, foam, and sweep across the sand, I was struck with a message from God. I heard a voice within me say, 'There is nothing but life!'"

And she said, "I knew then where my son was! I knew where my daughter was, and where my husband was!" For the first time, she was able to feel a sense of peace. And then she was able to start building her life again.

GOD GIVES US COMPANIONSHIP

"Blessed are those who mourn, for they shall be comforted." They get courage . . . enough to make it through a

Never look
at what you
have lost

Look at
what you
have left

funeral—or whatever they are facing. They are given a sense of calm. And they get another big "C"—companionship. In my thirty-three years as a pastor, I have heard the same comment over and over again from people who have had a devastating experience. They say, "Oh, we received so many telephone calls and letters. I heard from people I hadn't heard from in years. I was amazed at how many people care about me."

I'll never forget the funeral where no one came. The deceased man had three sons. All of them lived right there in this town. Yet none of them attended their father's funeral. Only the mortician and I were there.

I said, "What is wrong? Where is everybody?" The mortician said, "He was a very, very selfish man. In his life he never had time for his family; little wonder they have no time for him now."

There's a condition to the promises I'm sharing with you today. The promise, "Blessed are those who mourn, for they shall be comforted" does not apply to any and all persons. Remember the question to which I'm speaking in this chapter is, "What happens to *good* people when bad things happen to them?"

When my daughter Carol had her accident and lost her leg, nothing meant more to her than the photo she received from John Wayne. He signed it, "Dear Carol: Be happy; you're loved."

I tell you, that one sentence made as deep an impression

on me as it did on Carol. You can accept a great loss if you have somebody loving you through it. God will send you friends.

Keith Miller is a theologian, philosopher, and psychologist who, along with people like Bruce Larson, helped establish what has been called relational theology. His ministry through the years has been to interpret the teachings of Jesus Christ in a way that helps people become healthy. Over a million copies of his book, *The Taste of New Wine,* have been sold.

Keith enjoyed the success, the love, and the admiration that came to him as a result of his ministry. But then he went through the sorrow of a painful divorce. He felt like a failure and, regrettably, some Christians wrote him off, saying, "How could you be a Christian if you've had a divorce?" But then many, including people whom he'd helped, came to him and said, "How can we love you?" Through all their support he was able to feel and understand the reality of grace.

Now he has a whole new ministry to others who are hurting and are finding real power because they've given up on their own power. They're finding real love.

What happens to good people when they go through bad times? They can find companions who will love them and support them. A new love will come into their lives. They will find a sense of courage and a center of calm relief, hope, and peace that they never knew existed before.

GOD GIVES US COMPASSION

Courage, calm, companionship . . . and compassion. Every good person who goes through bad times develops a greater sensitivity. There's a marvelous line I've quoted often: "In love's service, only broken hearts will do." Good people turn their scars into stars.

Dr. Benjy Brooks is a great woman. She has been the recipient of the Horatio Algier Award and also has the distinction of being the first woman pediatric surgeon in the United States. She holds the position of Professor of Surgery at the University of Texas Medical School in Houston, Texas, and Special Assistant to the President in Ethics.

When Dr. Brooks was in the fifth grade, her teacher told her mother that she was mentally retarded. Benjy says today that she just marched to a different drummer. She said, "I didn't really fit into that sausage mill, to come out a little sausage like everybody else. Unfortunately, that's what our educational system does to children. At times, it takes away their creativeness and the fact that they are different."

But Benjy was determined to be a doctor. In fact, she was often found under the kitchen table "operating" on her sister's dolls with manicure scissors. And she was not about to let a teacher or an educational system stand in her way.

Then something happened that had a profound effect on Benjy and her medical practice. Her only brother, a test pilot in the Air Force, was killed at twenty-seven years of age.

And so she grieved. She says about her grief, "I don't think you get over it. You learn to live with it. And I learned to live with my brother's death. Later, in my medical practice, I saw him *at every age* as the little boys, then older boys, came through. I was able to love them and give to them instead of him."

GOD GIVES US A NEW SET OF COMMITMENTS

How does God comfort good people when bad things happen to them? He gives them courage, companionship, and compassion. He also gives them a new set of commitments. One of the best examples of this is Art Linkletter.

I count it an honor to call Art a friend. His humor and delightful way of looking at American life has brought joy and laughter into all our lives. But when you look beyond Art's wit and optimism you see a man who has turned his cross into a commission—a commitment to reach the lives of young people who are ensnared in the deathtrap of drugs. All of this grew out of his daughter's tragic death as a result of drugs and his son's death in an automobile accident.

I asked him once, "Art, how do you turn a tragedy into a personal triumph?"

He answered me in his warm, wise, loving manner, "The most difficult thing is to admit the tragedy, to accept it. It is something in your life over which you had no control, and

God's plan for us, as we all know, is more than we can fathom. It's part of the pattern of life—life and death.

"Having once admitted and accepted the deep, deep pain of the wound, then you begin to realize that you have expanded your own capability of loving and caring for others. Until you are hurt, you can never truly understand the hurts of others. Until you have failed, you cannot truly achieve success. In my own case, the pain in my life started me on a crusade against drug abuse—trying to help young people and families.

"Not everybody may be called to start a crusade as I was, but everybody can reflect love and caring. Every person's life touches some other life that needs love today."

I agree. "In love's service only broken hearts will do."

People facing tragedy suddenly take a new look at their whole life. Their whole perspective changes. Some of the things they had thought were so precious don't seem to mean much anymore. Some of the treasures they valued so highly don't seem as valuable. Their value system changes. And believe me, when your value system changes, your heart changes, your mood changes, your mind changes. Your life and your relationships change.

I remember calling on the home of a very rich woman who had suffered a great personal tragedy. This woman owned vases from China—from the Ming Dynasty—she had jewels and many other beautiful and valuable things. She greeted me and said, "Dr. Schuller, I heard you say once on television, 'Trouble never leaves you where it found you.' That is so true."

She said, "These things I own don't mean nearly as much to me now. Oh, I still love them; I'm not going to throw them away. But if there was a fire and I could save just one thing in the house, I wouldn't take that Ming vase now, as I would have before. Do you know what I'd take? I'd take the family pictures."

When tragedy hits, values change. Family becomes more important—husband, wife, parents, children. Relationships become more precious, and life itself more important than any day-to-day occupation or any material possession. When your values change, your life changes. And that's why the people that mourn are really comforted. Believe it or not, they're happy.

"I'M GOING TO REMAIN COOL, CALM, AND CORRECTED."

Blessed are the meek, for they shall inherit the earth.

BLESSED ARE THE meek, for they shall inherit the earth." Doesn't that sound ridiculous?

We live in a high-powered country called the United States of America. Don't we all know that it is the high-energy, powerful promoter— the big wheeler-dealer—who gets ahead?

"Blessed are the *meek,* for they shall inherit the *earth*." If Jesus had said, "Blessed are the meek, for theirs is the kingdom of heaven"—*that* we could understand. But to say that the meek shall inherit the *earth* sounds a little ridiculous to our ears, as finely tuned as they are to popular theories of success.

What was Jesus teaching when He said, "Blessed are the meek, for they shall inherit the earth"? Does this verse mean we are never to speak up and defend ourselves? Injustices do occur in our society. We live in a world where there are prejudices. How do you handle them? Does this verse mean we should allow ourselves to be doormats, letting people trample over us?

I am reminded of a story that my Catholic friend, Father Joseph Murphy, told me about some nuns who attended a baseball game. Behind the nuns sat some anti-Catholics. One anti-Catholic said very loudly, for the benefit of the nuns, "Let's go to Texas; I hear there aren't many Catholics there."

His companion replied, "Let's go to Oklahoma; there are even fewer Catholics there."

And the first one said, "Let's go to Alaska; there are almost no Catholics there."

At that point, the nun turned around and said, "Why don't you go to hell? There aren't any Catholics there."

"Blessed are the meek." Does this mean we must quietly accept insults and injustice with unlimited forbearance? Well, if we go back to the original Greek and examine the word that was originally translated as "meek," we see how misconception arises concerning this Bible verse.

The word *meek* is really not a good translation in terms

of modern usage; it meant something different four hundred years ago in Old England, when the King James translation was done, than it does today. A better modern translation of the verse might be, "Blessed are the mighty, the emotionally stable, the educable, the kindhearted, for they shall inherit the earth." This is the person who will be successful and "inherit the earth."

"Meek"—what does it mean? The answer lies in the word itself:

    M—Mighty

    E—Emotionally stable

    E—Educable

    K—Kind

BLESSED ARE THE MIGHTY

I can hear the protests now: "Wait a minute! Did you say, 'Blessed are the *mighty*'? How in the world can you substitute *mighty* for *meek*? You've gone too far this time, Schuller!"

Oh, but you *can* read this verse, "Blessed are the mighty." Think of it. What is real strength? What is real might? Who is the stronger—the young man who gives in to his rage and becomes physically or verbally abusive? Or the young man who remains calm, assured of his inner strength?

Who are the mighty? The powerful are mighty when they have learned to restrain their power. They know that real might lies in control and discipline, lest they rip out young plants along with weeds and tear out the tender shoots of human kindness and gentleness. They are those who remain gentle while they build strength, who are merciful while they are mighty. Blessed are they, for they shall not merely win a war; they shall win the hearts of a nation!

The weak are also mighty when they turn their problems into projects, their sorrows into servants, their difficulties into dividends, their obstacles into opportunities, their tragedies into triumphs, their stumbling blocks into stepping stones. They look upon an interruption as an interesting interlude. They harvest fruit from frustration. They convert enemies into friends! They look upon adversities as adventures.

I will never forget the 1982 New York City Marathon—not because of the winner, but because of the girl who came in last. Linda Down and her twin sister were born twenty-eight years ago with cerebral palsy. As a result of that condition, they were left with a lack of motor coordination and balance, as well as muscle spasticity. They can only walk with the assistance of special crutches. Yet Linda Down inspired me as well as all of America when she completed a marathon run—26.2 miles—on crutches!

For a disabled person to dream of running in the New York City Marathon may seem to be an unintelligent goal. But Linda's no dummy. In fact, she's a licensed social worker with a Master's degree. So I asked her, "Whatever inspired you to try getting into a marathon?" She replied, "Well, I guess part of it was wanting to test myself and see if I could actually do it. I always thought I couldn't because I was disabled. Part of it was because I had been unemployed. I wanted to try and make some kind of a positive statement that would help people. I thought that if I could do this, then it would help people to feel that they would be able to do things in their life that they were afraid of trying, because they felt it was impossible.

"It took a whole year to prepare for the marathon, and there were times when I really thought I'd never make it. My longest training session on the street was seven hours. That gets very long after awhile—just running for seven hours. I'd think, 'I'm going to make an idiot of myself.' But I hung in there till the end and I did it! I made it! I ran the entire 26.2 miles.

"I guess I just wanted to do it very badly. And I figured that no one really expected me to get more than two feet, so however far I got would be a success for me. I didn't know at the beginning if I'd be able to make it all the way to the end but I made a promise that God could take me as far as He wanted me to go and I would keep going until I just couldn't stop. And we made it!

"It took me eleven hours and fifty-four seconds to finish the marathon. That's a record I don't think anybody's going to break for awhile!

"A number of people have approached me on the street since the marathon and have congratulated me. One woman in particular stands out in my mind. She told me she had been in a deep depression prior to seeing me run the marathon. But she said that ever since she saw me she had been unable to forget my face. And because of what I was able to do, she thought maybe she could start to come out of this depression she's been in."

Linda Down, a victim of cerebral palsy, ran an entire marathon, and she's inspired millions! She's found the secret of happiness. What is it? It's her attitude—her Be-Happy Attitude: "If I attempt the impossible in my condition, perhaps I can inspire others to be happy and successful too."

What is a Be-Happy Attitude? In part, it is being able to harness my handicap and use it to pull others out of the ditch of depression! It is this: "Blessed are the meek—blessed are those who are strong enough to turn their tragedies into triumphs!"

BLESSED ARE THE EMOTIONALLY STABLE

Who are the emotionally stable? They are those who through discipline have developed a divine poise. They hold their negative impulses in check. They avoid and resist distractions and temptations which would excite and stimulate, but which drain their financial, moral, and physical resources.

People who *don't* control their emotions will permit themselves to fall into deep discouragement and depression. They'll quit and walk away from it all. Then they'll say later on, "I wish I could go back, but I can't. They won't have me back, because I walked away from it when it got difficult. They don't want that kind of person."

Blessed are the emotionally stable. They have their ups and downs, but they don't allow their down times to distract them from their goals. They don't quit when they hit their first snag, their first setback. They hang in there for the entire count, rather than throw in the towel after a low blow.

The meek are emotionally stable. They are those who have the strength to resist temptation, and it is only those who have this inner strength who will finally succeed. There are many, I'm afraid, who are too easily persuaded by a flashing star, the loud music, the bugle call to seek excitement. Too often, people lack restraint and get caught up in cultural fads. They waste their time chasing shooting stars.

Blessed are the honest, hardworking folks. They are more interested in substance than in style. They are more concerned about character building than about popularity rating. They are more dedicated to making solid achievements than to running after swift but synthetic happiness.

The emotionally stable stick to their objectives. They keep their eyes focused on their goals. And when they meet with problems, they patiently overcome those problems and work through their difficulties. More than one person has reached the top because he patiently endured difficult times. He might have been tempted to turn and run, or to lash out at the person who hurt him. But he didn't. More than one person has suffered through a time of stress in the company, in his marriage, with the children, and patience has paid off.

In the New Testament (Luke 18:15), Jesus tells a story to teach the people the value of patience and encourage them not to lose heart. A certain widow sought protection from her enemy. She went to the judge of her city time and again. At first the judge, who "did not fear God or respect man," turned a deaf ear to her pleas. However, she implored him over and over until he finally gave her the legal protection she needed.

The meek are patient. And the patient will inherit the earth. A modern-day example of patience and the reward it brings is a young lady whom I have grown to respect and admire. Her name is Lisa Welchel. Many of you know her as Blair, the snobby rich girl on the television series, *The Facts of Life*.

Many of you would say that Lisa has "inherited the earth." She is successful, famous, wealthy, beautiful, and talented. But most of all, she is respected and admired by her peers and her colleagues.

If you are familiar with the fictional character, Blair, you'd think, "Come on, Schuller, she may have inherited the earth, but Blair is anything but meek." True, Blair is not meek. But Lisa is. She embodies the original meaning of this

Beatitude. For Lisa is "meek" in that *she knows where her strength and success comes from.*

Lisa got her start when she was seven years old. She read that auditions were being held for the Mickey Mouse Club, so she wrote and asked if she could audition. She was told that the auditions had already been held and the show had been cast. But Lisa didn't quit. She wrote lots and lots of letters. Her final letter said, "I'm a Christian, and I feel that Disney is the only place I can work right now because the context of other shows is not what I could represent. I would really appreciate a chance to audition. I would be willing to fly myself out there." Disney agreed to give Lisa a chance. They liked her, and she got the part. From there, she got the part of Blair, who is really very different from Lisa.

Lisa is a charming, delightful girl who lives and works in Hollywood, which many would say is a difficult if not impossible place for a beautiful, young, single girl to retain old-fashioned values and Christian behavior. I asked Lisa about this, and here's what she said: "Well, you know, I feel that all the values the Lord has laid down for us are really for our own benefit. And if we think that we want to do something contrary to those values, well, that's fine, but we're only going to be hurting ourselves if we give in. God knows the future, and He knows why He set down certain rules. I feel that the Lord is just. Like He says, He's our Father and He's looking out for us. So long as I can remember that God's rules are only for my good and for my own happiness, and that He knows better than I do, then they are easy to adhere to."

Lisa knows the secret to happiness. And let me tell you something—a girl who keeps herself pure in private life has a warmth radiating from the eye that is just totally opposite from the hard look some people pick up. She is so bubbly, so enthusiastic. I asked her, "Lisa, where do you get your enthusiasm, your love for life?" Her answer was psychologically and theologically sound. She said, "It's from knowing that I am loved no matter what, and that I don't have to perform and I don't have to be a good person. I don't even have to follow the Lord's laws to be loved. It's just total grace and it's all mercy. It's knowing that I'm loved just because He created me. So if I blow it, I blow it, but Jesus is still standing here with open arms. And if I do good He's standing there to commend me. When you know you're totally accepted for who you are, it's a lot easier to be yourself with others. If they accept me, that's great, but if they don't, that's okay, too, because then I'll just run home to Daddy—to Jesus, to my Heavenly Father."

"Blessed are the meek." Blessed are the emotionally stable—the patient, the persistent—for they shall inherit the earth. They shall make it. They shall see their God-given dreams come true.

There is a success principle that I call the laminated principle. It works like this: You make a promise—and deliver. You accept an assignment—and fulfill it. You attempt

Passionate
persistence without
impertinence
produces
progress!

something "impossible"—and pull it off. Finally, year after year, maybe decade after decade, you have applied one accomplishment on top of another, one achievement over another—promises kept and commitments fulfilled. Your reputation is like a laminated beam that has durability and power. People believe in you. They take you at your word. They'll sign a contract with you because they know you're going to deliver. At that point you've "inherited the earth." Blessed are the patient people, blessed are the persistent. They shall ultimately win.

BLESSED ARE THE EDUCABLE

If we were to examine the original Greek of the Beatitudes, we would see that when Jesus said "Blessed are the meek," He could have meant, "Blessed are the *educable* for they shall inherit the earth." Educable people—those who are teachable—don't suffer from a "know it all" attitude. They allow room in their life for growth. They listen. They're not defensive. They're not on an ego trip. Rather, they are on a success trip. If their way isn't the best, they'll switch. Blessed are the teachable, for they shall succeed.

Blessed are those who know what it is that they do not know, and who are eager to listen to others who are older, wiser, more experienced. Blessed indeed are they who, in true meekness, remember that a little learning is a dangerous thing. Blessed are those who never forget they are never too

76

old to learn. They shall inherit great wisdom and, with it, success.

The educable are humble as well as teachable. Humility doesn't mean to put yourself down, to say, "I'm nobody. I can't do it." That's not humility. It may be an acquired, learned behavioral response imposed by a culture or a faith. It may be the projection of an inferiority complex. But real humility is not self-denigration. Real humility is the awareness that there are others who can help you. Real humility is also the capacity to say, "I was wrong; you were right."

Real humility is the ability to say, "I don't want my way if I'm wrong. I don't want my own way if it will prove to be a mistake."

Look at the alternative. How far does a cocky, know-it-all person really get? Not too far. And if he's able to somehow achieve his goals through thievery or manipulation, his ill-gotten gains will only feed his destructive attitude, and this is certain to produce unhappiness.

Jesus said it: "What shall it profit a man, if he shall gain the whole world, and lose his own soul?" (Mark 8:36, KJV).

Who are the meek? They are the people who begin by saying in true humility, "God has something for me. What is it?" Humility isn't thinking less of yourself; it is thinking more of God and of His dream for you. To be meek is to do God's work in His way, wherever you are.

I recently had the joy of speaking at Dunbar High School in Washington, D.C. This school happens to be in the inner-city of Washington. There are probably four hundred or five hundred young people in that school. I was thrilled to be there because Dunbar High School bears the name of a man who is one of my favorite poets, Paul Lawrence Dunbar. I said to these shining, eager faces, "Have you heard these lines written by that great black poet, Paul Lawrence Dunbar?"

> *The Lord had a job for me,*
> *But I had so much to do,*
> *I said, "You get somebody else,*
> *Or wait til I get through."*
> *I don't know how the Lord came out,*
> *But He seemed to get along.*
> *But I felt kind of sneakin' like—*
> *Knowed I'd done God wrong.*
>
> *One day I needed the Lord—*
> *Needed Him right away;*
> *But He never answered me at all,*
> *I could hear Him say,*
> *Down in my accusin' heart:*
> *"Brother, I'se got too much to do;*
> *You get somebody else,*
> *Or wait til I get through."*
>
> *Now, when the Lord he have a job for me,*
> *I never tries to shirk;*

I drops whatever I have on hand,
And does the good Lord's work.
And my affairs can run along,
Or wait til I get through;
Nobody else can do the work
That God marked out for you.

Be open. Be humble. Correctable. Educable. Then you will hear God's voice. You will see God's plan. Grab onto it, give it all you've got, and you will inherit the earth!

BLESSED ARE THE KIND

This is the final key to understanding what Jesus meant when He said, "Blessed are the meek." Without kindness the mighty are ruthless. Without kindness the emotionally stable are emotionally cold and hard. Without kindness the educable become arrogant.

The truly meek person is mighty, emotionally stable, educable—*and* kind. Without kindness we have only M-E-E, which is significant, for without kindness we are self-centered and surely doomed to failure and unhappiness. The M-E-E attitude is an Un-Happy Attitude. The M-E-E-K attitude is a Be-Happy Attitude.

Who are the kind people? They are the *sensitive spirits*. Happy indeed is the heart which is sensitive to another's

*I'd rather
change my
mind . . . and
succeed! Than have
my own
way . . . and
fail.*

insecurity. Loving is he who offers reassurance to another's hostility, affection to another's loneliness, friendship to another's hurt, and apologies to all. Blessed are such sensitive souls, for they shall inherit the devotion and esteem of good people on this earth!

I met several of these sensitive spirits—about one hundred eighty-five of them—at a school in Long Beach, California. It is the Florence Nightingale School for the mentally retarded. Clyde Thompson, the principal at the time of my visit, and Larry Bruns, a member of the staff, were members of my congregation. They invited us to visit the school. It was an unforgettable experience.

The mentally retarded fall into three classifications. In the highest classification are the educable. They are only slightly retarded and have the mental capacity to actually earn a high-school diploma. They can go out into society and most people will never know that they are slightly retarded.

By contrast, in the lowest classification are those who are apparently incapable of any formal education—the hydrocephalic, the huge-headed children, and the microcephalic, the tiny-headed children.

In the middle category are the Down's Syndrome children and many others. Many of these may learn to read or count, and almost all understand pictures.

Going through this school was a fantastic experience. While I was on my tour, at least twenty children stopped Mr. Thompson as Mrs. Schuller and I were walking with him.

They would run up to him and say, "Mr. Thompson, look—I did it all by myself." Over and over we heard this same sentence. "Look, I did it all by myself."

Clyde Thompson and his staff are sensitive spirits. They have built upon the strengths in these children and helped them feel pride, self-esteem, achievement. And the students themselves are sensitive spirits. In the Florence Nightingale School they record no problems of violence, street fighting, knifing, or kicking. You do not see scribbling on the walls.

If somebody loses a pencil or a coin on the playground, the first child who finds it will run to the principal's office and say, "Here, I found this on the grass." There is no stealing.

Everyone in that school from the age of six through twenty-one years learns to do *something*—nobody fails. They are taught to be creative—to weave, to sew, to print, or to draw. When they finish school, there is a factory down the street where they are all hired and can work. I watched as some graduates of the school filled an order for a commercial firm which made garden hoses. They needed to put six washers in a little plastic bag. It was set up like an assembly line.

How do the administrators make sure that retarded children who can't count will put exactly six washers in each plastic bag? Simple! The educators have developed a little piece of wood which is about one inch high. The children are told to put enough washers on that wood to reach the top. When this happens, they empty the washers into the plastic bag. The peg holds just six washers. So they never make a miscount. They work a full day; they do not complain. They have the Be-Happy Attitude, and they are beautiful persons!

I left that school surrounded by a mental environment of love, good-will, creativity, and self-esteem: "I did it all by myself!"

"Blessed are the meek." And the meek are the kind people, the sensitive spirits. They build up those around them. They are also the *quiet* people. They do so much good for so many without fanfare, glory-seeking, or headline-hunting. They shall inherit the trust, respect, and love of the truly beautiful people on this earth!

It's been nearly twenty-five years since I buried Rosie Gray in a simple ceremony in a cemetery in the little town of El Toro, California.

I had started my church in that town in a drive-in theater, for want of a better place. And on the first Sunday a California rancher lifted his paralyzed wife into his car to take her to this new "drive-in" church. Then came the day when he telephoned me and asked me to call on his wife in their home.

I will never forget Warren Gray, her husband, meeting me outside his little ranch house and saying, "Reverend Schuller, before you meet my wife I must tell you something about her. You might think she does not have her senses, but her mind is perfect, absolutely perfect. She has had a stroke, and she cannot raise her head. She cannot close her eyes and she cannot move them; they simply stare ahead. Her head just stays on her chest. She cannot walk; she cannot talk. She can cry a little and grunt a little, but that is all."

I went into the house. She sat slumped in an old over-stuffed chair, her head resting with her chin on her chest. Her eyes were open wide; they never blinked! I knelt in front of her so my eyes could make contact with hers, and I asked her, "Rosie, do you love Jesus?" A tear formed and rolled down her cheek. "Rosie, do you want to be baptized?" A couple more tears rolled down and she grunted, "Uh, uh, uh."

The following Sunday Warren parked their car in the front row of the drive-in. I attached a long drop cord to my microphone, walked over to her car, and, reaching through an open window, baptized her.

At that time our church was ready to move into a beautiful chapel that we had just built on two acres of land. What were we going to do now about Rosie Gray? The drive-in setting had been perfect for her needs.

The decision was made to have services at 9:30 in the new chapel. Then I would go back to the drive-in to preach to Rosie in her car. I would do that for her until she passed away. "That won't be long," we all thought. But she lived one year, two years, three years, four years, five years—she just would not die. Amazing!

Finally, God put into our minds His Dream for a most unusual church. Why not design a building where walls

84

Blessed are
those whose
dreams are
shaped
by their hopes,
not by
their hurts!

would open and people in their cars could join inside-the-church worshipers in prayer and praise?

So, we bought a larger piece of property and designed such a church. We had the groundbreaking ceremony on a Sunday. The local newspapers ran the story on Monday morning—the ground had been broken for what was called the world's first walk-in, drive-in church. On that same afternoon I had a funeral . . . for Rosie Gray.

Today the Crystal Cathedral where my congregation meets has walls that open to drive-in worshipers. And I shall always know that our unique church would not be the way it is had it not been for Rosie Gray! She was a quiet, meek soul, but she had a big impact on the direction of my ministry.

The kind people are the sensitive spirits. They are the quiet people, through whom God can do so much. They are also those who are *willing to be third*. Happy, indeed, are the people who are willing to put Jesus first, others second, and themselves third in line. Richly rewarded in this life are those who learn the lesson of our Lord that if any man would be master, he should learn to be a servant:

> "Whoever would be great among you must be your servant, and whoever would be first among you must be your slave" (Matt. 20:26, 27).

> "He who finds his life will lose it, and he who loses his life for my sake will find it" (Matt. 10:39).

The kind people are the sensitive spirits, they are the quiet people, and they are willing to be third. But most importantly, they are *God-shaped, Christ-molded* people.

I shall always treasure a marvelous picture that I received from Bishop Fulton Sheen when he was still alive. Inscribed on it are these words: "To my dear friend, Dr. Robert Schuller," and then this text:

> *Some come in chariots,*
> *Some on horses,*
> *but we come in the name of the Lord.*

Yes, blessed are those people who come not with a big splash and a lot of show, but humbly, honestly, carrying the Word of the Lord.

It begins to make sense, doesn't it?

"Blessed are the meek, for they shall inherit the earth."

Of course! Consider it by its contrast. Cursed are the cocky, the arrogant, the haughty and boastful, for they will have few friends! Unhappy are the elbowing, crowding, shoving, pushing, get-out-of-my-way, I'm-first bullies; they shall make many enemies! Headed for failure are the know-it-all Joes. Deaf to constructive criticism, careless of shrewd counsel, and indifferent to warnings, they are headed for a fall!

Doomed are the hot-heads! Unhappy are they who lose their cool and are too proud to say, "I'm sorry." They will never inherit the earth. They will not even hold their job, or perhaps their husband or wife. Hell-bent on this earth are the impatient, restless, rootless, ruthless promoters. They may gain a crown and lose the kingdom! "What shall it profit a man, if he shall gain the world, and lose his own soul?"

"Blessed are the meek, for they shall inherit the earth." This Be-Happy Attitude is beginning to sound like the best advice ever offered.

Indeed, it is true. In the long pull those who win the world around them are those whom Jesus calls the "meek"— the controlled; the patient; the honest; the quiet; the forceful; the powerful-but-restrained, disciplined, poised people. The God-molded, Christ-shaped, Holy-Spirit-dominated lives are like a train that will make many a "happiness stop."

Look at the ultimate example of the truly "meek"— look at Jesus Christ:

He was controlled emotionally:
He was spat upon,
   insulted,
      stripped,
         ridiculed,
            despised.

He was led as a lamb to the slaughter.
   Yet he never struck back!

FOOLISH?
He inherited the earth,
didn't He? There's not
a land where He is
not loved!

He demonstrated quiet determination:
 Steadfastly, He set His face to Jerusalem.
 He knew what He had to do. And He did it!

RIDICULOUS? INSANE?
He inherited the earth,
didn't He? Men of every
color and national origin
kneel before him!

He was gentle, kind, forgiving, loving—
 even to those who killed Him.

STUPID! you say. WAS IT?
He could face God with a clear conscience
when He died!
"It is finished," He said. And today
the world loves Him!

His enemies? They are the truly dead. But Christ lives on! Harry Kemp wrote:

I saw the Conquerors riding by
With cruel lip and faces wan:
Musing on kingdoms sacked and burned
There rode the Mongol Genghis Khan;

And Alexander, like a God,
Who sought to weld the world in one;
And Caesar with his laurel wreath;
And like a thing from hell—the Hun;

And leading, like a star the van,
Heedless of up stretched arm and groan,
Inscrutable Napoleon went
Dreaming of empire and alone....

Then all perished from the earth
As fleeting shadows from a glass,
And, conquering down the centuries,
Came Christ, the Swordless, on an ass!

"Blessed are the meek, for they shall inherit the earth." Until you understand this Beatitude, which is rooted in being the same kind of person Jesus was, by accepting Him as your Lord and Savior, you will never discover the real secret of happiness. You will read this entire book and wonder why you are still unhappy, still depressed, still searching for something more.

Are you meek?

🍂 Are you *Mighty* enough to be controlled and disciplined?

🍂 Are you *Emotionally Stable* enough to resist temptation?

🍂 Are you *Educable* enough to realize you can't do it all by yourself?

🍂 Are you *Kind* enough to be sensitive, quiet, unselfish—Christ-molded?

If you are, you will have mastered the third of the Be-Happy Attitudes. You'll come to the end of your life with pride behind you, love around you, and hope ahead of you. Who could ask for more?

"I REALLY WANT TO DO THE RIGHT THING!"

Blessed are those who hunger and thirst for righteousness, for they shall be satisfied.

*M*OST OF US IN America don't know what it is to be hungry or thirsty. Right?

My daughter Sheila recently had to have some x-rays taken. She was told that the night before she could have only clear jello, clear broth, and a few glasses of water—and nothing after midnight.

At first, Sheila didn't think it would be too difficult to comply with the instructions. When she went out to dinner with her husband the night before the x-rays were to be taken, she felt a few pangs of disappointment when she looked at her cup of broth and then at his plate brimming with delicious food. A couple of times she instinctively reached out and took a chip from the basket in the middle of the table, only to realize she couldn't have it. "At that point," she later recounted, "I felt pangs of disappointment, but not hunger—not yet."

The next morning Sheila went to the office. Her stomach was starting to growl by now. She desperately craved a Danish pastry and a hot steaming cup of coffee. She couldn't wait for her test to be over so she could have something to eat and drink again.

She tried to work. Her mind was fuzzy, and she was feeling weak. She consoled herself: "I only have to wait one more hour, then the test will be over and I can eat again."

She drove herself to the hospital for the test, bothered now by a slight headache. The test was grueling and long, and before it was over her headache had become a throbbing migraine. When they told her the test was finished and that she could go home, she felt wobbly. She was having difficulty focusing. Her depth perception was giving her problems.

So she called her husband: "Jim, quick. I need you to take me to lunch."

It was amazing what eating a good meal did for her. "My strength came back," she told me later. "My headache left. My vision cleared." She added, "Dad, I felt real hunger and thirst today for the first time! Now I understand what happens to us when we don't give our bodies the nourishment they need."

So most of us in America never know what it is like to be hungry and thirsty. Right? Wrong! Almost all of us suffer from some kind of emotional and spiritual hunger.

Mother Teresa observed during one of her early visits to America, "In India—people are dying of physical starvation. In America—people are dying of emotional starvation."

Why are so many of us constantly restless in a pursuit of "something more"? Something is missing, we vaguely but strongly suspect, even when things are going well for us.

How can we understand, analyze, interpret, or explain the emotional restlessness that relentlessly pressures us to reach further, climb higher, acquire more? The result? The clock never stands still. We fail to fully enjoy the present moment. Our emotions are projected into the activities and events of tomorrow. So busy are we in our planning the future that we never taste the pleasures of the present.

"Once I hoped that I'd be wealthy enough to own my own home," a person who must remain nameless confided to me. "When that happened, I immediately wanted something more—a vacation place. By the time I acquired that second residence I found myself traveling so much I seldom was at home to enjoy my primary residence. The more I got, the less I enjoyed everything I had."

Nothing leads to more despair and frustration than that gnawing feeling that something's missing from your life. It's like getting up in the middle of the night and going to the refrigerator. You open it, not really knowing what you want. So you nibble at this, you try that, but nothing tastes good. You finally close the door and go back to bed still hungry—unsatisfied. Many of us are similarly unfulfilled emotionally.

The trouble is that too many of us spend our lives the way I used to spend my days off. For me, Monday has always been my one day in seven for rest. When my church was smaller and my schedule was less hectic, my wife and I would spend Monday as our day away from the office and the home. On these totally free days we would ask each other, "So, what shall we do today?"

We would bounce around various ideas, but either they didn't strike our fancy, or they were too costly or too imprac-tical. Finally, frustrated with our indecision, we often ended up getting in the car and just cruising. We had no particular destination in mind. We just set out, hoping we'd see some-thing that looked interesting or fun. Often, however, by the time we decided what it was we wanted to do, the day was too far spent. We'd blown the whole day.

How can you be sure that you won't blow the one life you have to live? How can you satisfy your heart's deepest hungers? Where does genuine satisfaction come from?

  🎻 Does the answer lie in *fame?*

  🎻 Is *success* the answer?

🔊 Does satisfaction come with *power*?

🔊 Does *sexual gratification* bring real satisfaction?

Let's look at each of these and in the process maybe we will discover what it is that we are missing.

DOES FAME SATISFY?

Jesus does not say, "Blessed are those who *seek after fame*, for they shall be satisfied."

I have a friend who is a household word in the entertainment business. He's still quite young, yet he was very famous early in life, when his television show enjoyed the highest ratings. He made a lot of money! He was in big demand. Then the ratings dropped, and as soon as they did, the network canceled his show. He has no other career. He has no other business. He has nothing to fall back on.

This young man has been trying to find something to do, but nothing clicks. He's really going through a terribly rough time. And my friend is not unique in his experience. He is but one of many entertainers who have experienced fame only to have the public turn its back on them. Fame is fleeting. It does not satisfy!

I have another friend in the entertainment business, Hugh O'Brian, that famous actor who played the legendary lawman, Wyatt Earp, on television. Hugh was far more fortunate than my other friend. Hugh has a way of saying it that I love. He said, "I found out very early in my business that no matter who you are and no matter what business you're in, all of us go through five stages in life. Let me put it to you this way. The first stage is: *Who is Hugh O'Brian?* This is where you begin your journey—when you sow the seeds for success.

"The second is: *Get me Hugh O'Brian.* That's when you have your first taste of success.

"The third stage is: *Get me a Hugh O'Brian type.* That's when you're really successful—when you are at the top of the ladder, when they can't afford you but they want somebody like you.

"The fourth stage is: *Get me a young Hugh O'Brian.* We all grow old. We'll all go through the fourth stage. It all depends on how you handle it. Stay active and productive during this period. Maintain a purpose.

"The fifth stage is: *Who is Hugh O'Brian?*

"Now, no matter who we are, we all began at stage one and we're all going to wind up eventually at stage five, back where we came from. All the success and the money in the world won't buy you more tomorrows when your time has come.

"Consequently, it's what you do between stage one and stage five that makes a difference in your life. It's extremely important early on to develop projects, hobbies, and an avocation that keeps you active. That way, no matter what stage you're at—you can have a PURPOSE in life."

Hugh O'Brian's purpose—his magnificent obsession—is a program he founded called the Hugh O'Brian Youth Foundation. Its purpose is simply to seek out, recognize, and reward leadership potential in high school sophomores, and provide annual state and international leadership seminars for these future leaders. The idea for the program was inspired after Hugh spent nine days in 1958 with Dr. Albert Schweitzer in Lambarene, Africa. That profound experience deeply affected Hugh.

One of Dr. Schweitzer's statements especially struck home. Dr. Schweitzer said, "The most important thing in education is to make young people think for themselves." He also told Hugh, "Everybody has the ability to create his own Lambarene. Everybody has the ability to be a teacher of tomorrow—to teach young people about their potential and how to use it."

As a result of Dr. Schweitzer's influence, Hugh O'Brian developed his program aimed at motivating high school sophomores. The purpose of the program is to teach this age group not only how to dream, but how to bring their dreams to reality. As Hugh put it: "Most people are preoccupied in sending delinquents to camp. The great majority of our youth are positive, but we only hear about the negative minority. I figured it was time to pat the good guys and gals on the back and show them that there are rewards for being responsible members of the community.

"I believe that our young people are the greatest natural

Sincere self-forgetting, sacrificial service to searching and suffering souls satisfies my self-esteem more than the stimulation of a celebrity status!

resource that this country has. We have tremendous untapped leadership potential among the high school students of our great America. In this program, all we're trying to do is to give these young people an opportunity to ask their questions, to find out what the realities of life and business are all about. We want to equip them beyond teaching them ABCs. We want to help them dream.

"I love what I'm doing! I have a pretty realistic philosophy. I would like to share it with you as I have with thousands of young people who have participated in our seminars. It is called 'The Freedom to Choose':"

> I do not believe that we are all created equal. Physical and emotional differences, parental guidance, varying environments, being in the right place at the right time all play a role in enhancing or limiting development. But I do believe every man or woman, if given the opportunity and encouragement to recognize his or her potential, regardless of background, has the freedom to choose in our world. Will an individual be a taker or a giver in life? Will he be satisfied merely to exist or will he seek a meaningful purpose?
> I believe every person is created as the steward of his or her own destiny with great power for a specific purpose to share with others, through service, a reverence for life in a spirit of love.

Through his program, Hugh O'Brian and his volunteers have put their arms around more than a million young people. Hugh O'Brian is satisfied. (Well, maybe not—fortunately, he's still reaching for the sky!) But his satisfaction didn't come merely through fame. It came from having a purpose, from giving back to the country he loves, through doing something worthwhile and never counting the cost—for Hugh does not get paid for this work; he is the ultimate volunteer.*

DOES SUCCESS SATISFY?

Fame doesn't satisfy. Neither does success. Tom Landry, the super-successful coach of the Dallas Cowboys, is successful. But more than that, he is *satisfied.* Surprisingly, he shared with me that his satisfaction doesn't come merely from winning football games, although he does feel it's important to try with all our might to be all that we can be.

In fact, Tom said that there is a slogan he keeps prominently displayed in the Cowboys' locker room: "The quality of a person's life is in direct proportion to his commitment to excellence." Tom went on to say, "I believe that very strongly. I believe that God gave us all talent to do whatever we want to do and He expects us to do the best we can. When you try to be the best you can, then success and winning take care of themselves.

"Confidence comes from knowledge. If you know your job well, then you'll have the confidence to do it well when

---

*For information about the Hugh O'Brian Youth Foundation, write to: 10880 Wilshire Blvd., Room 2121, Los Angeles, CA 90024.

you get out on the field. You've got to anticipate the positive element all the time, because once you start thinking about the negative possibilities—that you may miss the Super Bowl, or you may lose, you may be fired next week—such negative thinking drastically reduces your chances of achieving your best. And so we try to think positively."

Tom Landry is a success. He says that anybody can be a winner if he wants it bad enough, strives for it hard enough, actively seeks it out by learning all he can and working with all his strength. Of course, positive anticipation, feeding on good, clear, positive attitudes is essential.

If we hunger and thirst after positive attitudes, hard work, knowledge, and excellence, the odds of our winning rise astronomically.

But that's not what this Beatitude says, is it? It's not, "Blessed are those who hunger and thirst after righteousness, for they shall be winners."

No, the Beatitude says, "Blessed are those who hunger and thirst for righteousness, for they shall be *satisfied.*"

My conversation with Tom Landry didn't end with talk about winning. He went on to explain how he had found real satisfaction.

"I wanted to be a good football coach, so my whole life was absorbed in that. As I went up the ladder all the way to becoming a professional football player and winning world championships with the New York Giants (that's where I was before I joined the Cowboys), I discovered that after the excitement of winning or being successful, there was always an emptiness and a restlessness that stayed with me afterwards.

"I didn't understand that. I thought that somewhere along the way you ought to win a victory that would sustain you for the rest of your life. But I never discovered that kind of satisfaction until one time a friend asked me to attend a Bible study that met at a hotel in Dallas on Wednesday morning. I thought he was crazy because I knew the Christmas story and the Easter story and I'd been to church every Sunday. But he was a good friend, so I went. I remember it so well. We were reading in the Sermon on the Mount in Matthew, where Jesus said, 'Do not be anxious about your life, what you shall eat or what you shall drink, nor about your body, what you shall put on. Is not life more than food, and the body more than clothing? . . . Seek first God's kingdom and His righteousness, and all these things shall be yours as well' (Matt. 6:25, 33).

"Well, that was my first real discovery of the Bible! It was the first time I'd ever studied it. I went on to learn what the gospel of Jesus Christ is all about. As a result I accepted Christ—one year before I took over the Dallas Cowboys. I learned what St. Augustine meant when he said, 'Our hearts are restless, O God, until they find their rest in thee.'

"I found that the emptiness and the restlessness left me. I really realized two things, Dr. Schuller. I realized that you can go to church all your life and not be a Christian. I had never known that. I think the other thing I discovered was that life is a matter of priorities. Up until that point, football was my first priority in life; my family and God took a back seat. But once I accepted Christ as my Lord and Savior, I discovered that God was first in my life. That made all the difference in the world and it's been that way in my life ever since."

DOES POWER SATISFY?

Jesus didn't say, "Blessed are those who seek after fame," or "after success," or even "after power."

Chuck Colson, who was once one of the most powerful men in our country and then was imprisoned as a result of the Watergate scandal, is a living example of this: You cannot find happiness through power.

Chuck was not happy when he commanded great power influence. Instead, his power led to ruin and even imprisonment. But then Chuck Colson found Jesus and was born again. Today he has an active ministry going on in over three hundred sixty-five prisons in the United States and in twenty-one countries of the world. He has thirty thousand volunteers active in the United States, and some fifty-eight thousand inmates have graduated from his evangelistic and discipleship training programs inside the prisons. He says, "It is the greatest thrill in the world to be part of a movement of God's people raised up to bring the Good News that Jesus Christ can change lives in those dark dungeons we call prisons in America.

"I've been so close to those in the highest office in the world," he continues. "I've been in palaces; I've preached in great cathedrals around the globe but the greatest joy and fulfillment I've had is to be in prison on a grimy concrete floor with a burly convict who, in a flood of tears, gives his life to Jesus."

DOES SEXUAL GRATIFICATION SATISFY?

How do you really satisfy that inner emotional hunger? Jesus didn't say, "Blessed are those who seek fame, success, or power." Likewise, Jesus didn't say, "Blessed are those who seek sexual gratification."

I disagree with Freud, who contended that the heart's deepest passion or need is pleasure. Man's ultimate need is for a healthy sense of self-esteem, self-worth, a sense of sanctified, Holy-Spirit-induced pride. It's the glorious feeling that Adam and Eve had before they fell into sin. I once asked Dr. Joyce Brothers, the well-known psychologist, "Joyce, what are some of the most basic, deepest psychological needs that you see in human beings today?"

She replied, "I think that human beings need *love*. It doesn't have to be the love between a man and woman. It can be love of mankind. It can be love of God. William James said it so many years ago: 'The most important thing in life is to *live your life for something more important than your life.*' That's what happy people do.

"You know, we live in an age of miracle drugs," Dr. Brothers continued, "But the miracle that still does the most to lengthen life, to make it happy, is the oldest miracle we know. It is the miracle of love. And from a psychologist's point of view, I see that people who are good are happy. People who are happy are people who are good.

"Human beings are capable of so much. Again, psychologists have found that people use only ten percent of their ability. But there are some people who will not stop at that ten percent. They push the limits, to find out what they are capable of doing. Those are the happy people."

In my opinion, Dr. Joyce Brothers has a much better handle on man's needs than Freud did. What Dr. Brothers said to me reflected what I have always believed to be man's deepest need—love and a sense of self-esteem—not passion, not sexual gratification, not fame, and not power.

THE SECRET OF SATISFACTION

Satisfaction, happiness, fulfillment—all are as elusive and fleeting as shadows when we search for them through fame, success, power, or sexual gratification.

How then can we find satisfaction? Jesus said, "Blessed are those who hunger and thirst for *righteousness,* for they shall be *satisfied."* In this powerful sentence, Jesus shows us how we can satisfy the heart's deepest hunger, its deepest longing.

Jesus says the way to satisfaction and happiness lies in seeking righteousness.

Question: What is righteousness?

Righteousness is not merely avoiding temptation successfully. It goes beyond that. Allow me to quote from my book, *Self-Esteem: The New Reformation:* [*]

> We all know people who do not lie, kill, steal, commit adultery, yet they live a life of ease, comfort, and noninvolvement. They appear to be kind and gentle, and we are tempted to judge them to be "loving people." But real love is sacrificial commitment. Until these "good people" set God-glorifying goals, they are making no potentially creative and constructive commitments. If they take no daring risk in mission, they're good—but good for what? (p.112)

Righteousness is not absolute holiness or perfection, either. I don't believe Jesus is saying that a person who has an incurable compulsion to holy living will really be satisfied. If we had to live perfect, holy lives in order to be satisfied, we would be the most miserable of human beings, because we all make too many mistakes. We all commit sins. None of us is going to be perfect.

It is true that when we do make mistakes, when we do sin, we can ask for God's forgiveness. Is this the path to righteousness? Yes—if we understand the real meaning of true repentance. Allow me to quote again from my book, *Self-Esteem: The New Reformation:*

> Real repentance is a positive, dynamic and highly-motivated redirection of life . . . to a caring, risky trust which promises

---

[*] Waco, Texas: Word Books, 1982.

the hope of glory . . . through noble, human-need filling achievements . . . If the slate is washed clean of guilt, I am only half forgiven. I am not fully forgiven until I allow God to write his new dream for my life on the blackboard of my mind. (pp. 103–104)

Negative repentance is an Un-Happy Attitude; it will drain you of your enthusiasm. It says, "I am nothing. I am worthless. I am bad." Righteousness will not evolve from such negativity.

Positive repentance, on the other hand, says:

• "I'm sorry I didn't believe in God's dreams. From now on I will."

• "I'm sorry for not loving myself as much as the Lord did when He died on the cross for me. From now on I'll remember God loves me—and I will try to love me, too."

• "I'm sorry I was so selfish that I surrendered to the fear of failure; I didn't want people to laugh at me. From now on I'll attempt to do something great for God."

• "I now commit myself to righteousness! I will do the right thing. I will respond to the dreams God gives me—even if they seem impossible."

Righteousness comes through *real* repentance. And repentance is a twofold process: (1) It is saying *"No"* to the negatives, the temptations to do and be less than our best. (2) It is saying *"Yes"* to the positives—the good, the healthy. It is saying *"Yes"* to God's dream for you and me.

SAY *"NO!"* BY SAYING *"YES!"*

In order to be satisfied we need healthy nourishment. We need to be selective in what we feed our minds and our souls with. It's not easy in today's world when we're surrounded by "junk food" thoughts. By that I mean the negative attitudes, negative reactions, and negative responses that bombard us every day. We need to insulate ourselves against these negatives and diligently seek the positive, the good—righteous thoughts, righteous dreams, and righteous actions.

In such a negative-thinking world, we are constantly surrounded by negative vibrations. The most positive person you meet still has his negative attitudes. No person is one-hundred-percent positive. We are emotionally conditioned to negativity by the world in which we live. How do we break these hypnotizing, negative chains? How do we liberate ourselves from the imprisonment of negative thinking? How do we say "No" to the negatives, the temptations that will rob us of our happiness?

Say "No!" by saying "Yes!" Eliminate the negatives by sowing positives:

 ❦ A perfect farm, a profitable farm, a righteous farm is not a farm where there are no weeds growing. Rather, it is the farm that's planted with crops such as corn or pineapple and is bearing fruit.

 ❦ A perfect sheet of paper isn't a sheet of paper that has no mark on it, without scratch or flaw. No. The perfect paper is one that is filled with notes, thoughts, concepts, and ideas, a poem, an outline, or numbers that put together some creative possibility.

 ❦ A perfect communication between two people isn't the type of relationship in which there are no fights, no arguments, no cross words. Perfect communication is when both persons are able to open up and actually tell each other how they feel with respect and mutual esteem. Not silence, but creative, constructive, respectful conversation is righteousness in communication.

So, we cannot claim that we are striving after righteousness by making a list of "don'ts" and trying to abide with them. Hungering and thirsting after righteousness must mean more than that! It must mean desiring to live the positive kind of life that will bear fruit and do something beautiful for God. The psalmist says that the *righteous* man shall be "like a tree planted by streams of water, that *yields its fruit in its season,* and its leaf does not wither. In all that he does, he prospers."

Many of you may have seen the wonderful movie, *The Karate Kid*. Remember the tough blond kid who fought against the hero in the climax of the movie?

Imagine my amazement when I learned that Billy Zabka, the young actor who played this terribly mean kid, was a Christian, and a very fine young man.

I met him and asked him, "Billy, how could you be so mean in *The Karate Kid?*"

"That was just acting," he explained. "I am a Christian first and an actor second. In fact, my career as an actor wasn't really going anywhere. I began to think that maybe God didn't want me to be an actor at all. He's called me so close to Him that I thought maybe He wanted me to go into youth ministries. I love kids and I love camping. I'd rather be in the mountains than in a limousine!

"But on a summer camping trip with my church fellowship group, I shared with my friends that I wanted to be in a movie. I explained that it wasn't for me; it was for God. But I wasn't sure if that was what God really wanted.

"When I returned home, I found I was up for the role in *The Karate Kid*. I pulled up in front of Columbia Studios. Usually before these interviews I pray, 'God, I don't want to do this if there's going to be any sin. I don't want to do this if there's going to be any corruption on the set.'

Righteousness?
It is:
positive,
Faith-producing
people who are
actively pursuing
a God-given
dream!

"But this time, I prayed, 'Lord, I want to minister your Word and reach out to people and say you love them.'

"It was neat how when I gave up my dreams and said, 'I don't care about my dreams; I only care about *Your* dreams'—that's when He gave me the opportunity!

"The movie is successful and I don't go around trying to advertise Billy Zabka. I go around trying to show the love of God. Not preaching to them. Not telling them they're damned in hell. But just by being a Christian, just loving God."

Yes, Billy is a "righteous" man. I mean that in this sense of the word: He has said "No" to the temptations that would drag him down, including the temptation to shut himself off from those whose lifestyles were offensive to him. When Billy said "Yes," he would live for Jesus, including being a witness to others on the movie set, then he was able to bear fruit; he has the opportunity to be a light to millions who know him from his movie career.

Righteousness comes through positive affirmations:

&. "I'm a child of God!"

&. "I'm God's idea, and God only has good ideas!"

&. "I *want* to do it! I *can* do it! I *will* do it!"

&. "I'm going to take chances!"

When you say "Yes!" you will be living and trusting in God's promises. When you attempt the impossible you will discover that you will be filled with excitement! Enthusiasm! Energy! Youth! Happiness!

Righteousness is attempting to accomplish some beautiful possibility. Win or lose—the attempt will build your self-esteem. Succeed or fail—you can be sure of this—you will be able to live with yourself and not be ashamed, which means you can be proud that you tried.

That's the joy! That's the deep satisfaction! That is the great reward!

A dear friend of mine is Bill Dearden, chairman of the board of Hershey Foods Corporation. Bill was just a young boy back in the 1930s—an orphan. But he was fortunate to go to an orphan school started by Milton Hershey, the founder of the company.

Mr. Hershey had no children of his own, and he had had a terrible time growing up himself. He only had a fourth-grade education. He failed three times in business ventures, but he had the courage to keep on trying. The fourth time he started in business—a caramel company—he was very successful.

He sold his caramel business for a million dollars and started the chocolate company. Knowing that his wife could never have any children, he decided to start an orphan school.

It was at this school that Bill Dearden received most of his education. He went on to work in the company and eventually became the chairman of the board. He tells me that Mr. Hershey set the company up so that 51% is owned by the school. So a lot of the money the company makes goes back into the school.

I asked Bill, "How did you make it from being a little orphan boy in the streets of Philadelphia to being the top corporate chief and chairman of the board of one of America's most respected corporations?"

He replied, "God has always had an important spot in my life. I believe that through His love and direction all things are possible. I think He helped me along the way—guided me, and directed me—and I think He will do that for everyone if they are willing to believe in Him."

Mr. Hershey had a burning desire to do something good with his life. So did Bill Dearden. And so the positive chain of real righteousness goes on.

If you live in Minnesota, you probably know who Joe Sensor is. For those of you who don't live in Minnesota, Joe played tight end for the Minnesota Vikings football team. Joe is also a graduate of the Hershey School. He became my friend while on the team, and I had the joy of baptizing his beautiful baby in the Crystal Cathedral.

Joe, whose father had died when he was very young, was offered an opportunity to go to the Hershey School. He accepted the offer and found tremendous love and support there. Later, he was drafted by the Vikings and had tremendous success in football. As a result of his success, he was called to do about fifteen hundred speaking engagements in a period of six years.

Joe Sensor has geared himself and dedicated himself to help as many children and young people as he can. As he once told me, "Professional athletes have the greatest opportunity because kids look up so much to professional athletes. The mother and father can tell them not to do drugs, and their words won't have much effect. But if a professional athlete tells them not to do drugs, they cling to that advice; it gets through to them. I am a servant of other people. I think that this is the most important thing that I can do with my life."

Bill Dearden, Joe Sensor. Who knows how many other young people in the last two generations have been changed because Milton Hershey hungered and thirsted to do something good with his life?

This is righteousness! This is how to find happiness! But if righteousness is so great, why isn't everybody pursuing it? What holds people back? Why do people say "No" to the good things? Why do they say "No" to God? There are three possible reasons:

(1) First, people say "No" to God because *they do not know any better.* There are still a lot of people who are hung up on the idea that if you really get religion, really get converted, really get saved and become a Christian, you may go off the deep end and become a little nutty or kooky or freaky. There are others who have been turned off by contact with religious hypocrites or fanatics or—worse—by joyless, negative Christians. So these people steer away from religion,

never realizing what a happy life they can have when they commit their whole lives to Him.

Dwight Moody used to say, "People have just enough religion to make themselves miserable; they cannot be happy at a wild party and they are uncomfortable at a prayer meeting."

How true it is! Many people have just enough religion to be miserable, but not enough to enjoy it. And so often this is because they have no idea what Christian life is really like. Frankly, I do not blame those whose only impression of God is the negative witness some Christians give. No wonder they turn Him off! They just do not know any better.

(2) There is a second reason why some people say "No" to God: *They do not think they can say "Yes" to Him.* Lack of self-esteem holds them back. Their thinking is: "God is perfect and I surely know I am not; therefore, I do not think I should join up with Him." What these people don't realize is that God does not call us to be perfect; He just calls us to be willing! He doesn't expect us to be sinless, although He does expect us to say, "Lord, I am willing to try." It is far better to do something constructive imperfectly than to do nothing perfectly!

(3) The third reason some people say "No" to God is *they think they are not quite ready.* They have projects that they have not started, projects that are half finished, telephone calls to make, unanswered letters to write. When they get their desks cleared and have a chance to think, probably then they will turn to God. But right now they are just too busy.

The trouble is, there may not be a "later on." Do it now!

Do not let God wait. If you feel a positive, inspiring thought go through your mind today, there is only one way to answer it: "Yes, Lord."

Say it now. It is not going to hurt you. Right now, lay this book on your lap and say the words, "Yes, Lord." Repeat them out loud until they sound natural. "Yes, Lord! Yes, Lord! Yes, Lord!"

Do not be afraid of seeming overly dramatic or of being overly emotional; do not let any negative fear hold you back. Say it strongly, positively: "Yes, Lord." I predict that within an hour a positive thought will come into your mind. A positive mood will begin to creep over you. When that happens, do not say, "No." Say again, "Yes, Lord."

Perhaps you will receive an invitation to turn your life over to Christ. If you have never yet made a commitment of your life to Jesus Christ, accepting Him as your Savior and your Lord, your personal, living friend, I invite you to do so! If you have not committed your life to Christ, take this positive step today. Doing so will turn you into a better person, not a worse person.

"Blessed are those who hunger and thirst for righteousness, for they shall be satisfied."

Are you satisfied? Are you happy? Is life all that you hoped it would be? It can be—it *will* be—if you will say "Yes" to the dream that God has given you.

🍃 Go for it! You might make it!

🍃 Go for it! It might happen!

🐚 Go for it! Somebody might be helped by it!

🐚 Go for it! You might rise from poverty to prosperity!

🐚 Go for it! If you prosper, you might be able to help the poor!

🐚 Go for it! Someday, somebody will come to you and say, "Thank you!"

That's satisfaction. It comes when you know you are worthwhile, that you are a valuable person, that you have made a contribution, a difference.

Hunger and thirst mean "Go for it!"

"They shall be satisfied" means that they can have the assurance that they have helped someone, they have made a difference, their lives have counted for something—something GREAT!

"I'M GOING TO TREAT OTHERS THE WAY I WANT OTHERS TO TREAT ME."

*I*N THIS BE-HAPPY Attitude is a sure prescription for happiness.

Blessed are the merciful, for they shall obtain mercy.

Learn to live by this refreshing happy attitude: "It's not what happens to me that matters most; it's how I react to what happens to me."

Be sure of this: If you have the attitude that you should forever be spared from all pain, hurt, and grief, you can be positive that someday you will be jolted with a depressing disillusionment. Sorrow, rejection, bereavement hit all of us at some point in our lives. To expect that somehow we are privileged persons and should be immune from hurt and hardship is unrealistic.

Some even feel, "Because I am a Christian, I should experience no pain and suffering. Because I'm a God-fearing person and a good person, I should experience no rejection or ridicule." If this is our attitude, we will react to adversity with self-pity. "It's not fair!" will be our immediate negative reaction. But the quicker we learn that life is not always fair, the sooner we can achieve emotional maturity.

We all have our share of suffering. And we all have two choices when we face a terrible experience. We can choose the Be-Happy Attitude, or we can choose the Un-Happy Attitude.

The Un-Happy Attitude is the way of anger and vengeance: "Revenge!" "I'll get even!" This negative attitude is a sure prescription for misery and unhappiness. People who are obsessed with fighting battles cannot be filled with joy. Their only satisfaction is having the bitter taste of frustration released through their spiteful, vengeful behavior.

Probably more times than we'll ever know, the unhappiness of those who choose the Un-Happy Attitude is multiplied through the breakdown of their physical health—high blood pressure, heart trouble, strokes, even cancer—produced by stress. This is the result of their choice of an Un-Happy Attitude toward unfortunate circumstances.

But there is an alternative attitude we can choose as we move through life. The positive attitude that will prove to be a Be-Happy Attitude is an option that is open to every person. It is the way of mercy and forgiveness—choosing to react positively and hopefully to whatever negative experiences that may befall us.

The good news I have for you is: God promises mercy adequate enough to meet any tragedy.

Jesus promised in the fifth Beatitude: "Blessed are the merciful, for they shall obtain mercy." This Beatitude holds three things—first, a *promise;* second, a *power principle* that has universal application; and third, a *prescription* for happy living.

THE PROMISE

Many people in my congregation would testify to the truth of God's promise in this Beatitude. Their testimony is that when an unexpected tragedy hits, they have found the capacity to find happiness anyway. Now, that's not human nature. The natural tendency would be to get angry, bitter, and cynical—to say, "There is no God." When a person reacts positively to tragedy—that's a miracle. Psalm 23 concludes with the glorious line: "Surely goodness and mercy shall follow me all the days of my life." That's God's way of saying that life will often be filled with goodness, but that even when God's goodness cannot be seen, His mercy can be experienced! In the midst of tears, heartbreak, enormous loss, and terrible sorrow, suddenly a sweet mood, like a

*When God's
goodness cannot
be seen . . .
His mercy
can be
experienced!*

gentle kiss, will touch your wounded heart. That experience is called mercy. It comes as an expression of God's love.

Throughout the Scriptures God promises that He will be merciful to us:

> "His mercy is on those who fear [trust] him" (Luke 1:50).

> "God, who is rich in mercy, out of the great love with which he loved us . . . made us alive together with Christ" (Eph. 2:46).

> "He saved us, not because of deeds done by us in righteousness, but in virtue of his own mercy" (Titus 3:5).

The promise is there! It is for you! What wonderful news! What wonderful assurance! No matter where our road will lead, no matter what pain may hit, no matter what we do, God will be there with His mercy to forgive us, to hold us up, and carry us through the tough times. But this is only half of the Beatitude: ". . . for they shall obtain mercy." The other half is, "Blessed are the merciful . . ."

The question is: Which comes first? Do we need to be merciful before God will be merciful to us? Or does God need to be merciful to us before we can be merciful to others? What did Jesus mean when He said, "Blessed are the merciful, for they shall obtain mercy"?

I believe Jesus meant:

🔹 God will be merciful to us.

🔹 Then we will be merciful to others.

🔹 Mercy will then come from a variety of sources.

The first step, then, is to accept God's mercy. All we need to do is *accept* the promise of the Beatitude. It is God's promise that if we treat people mercifully, God will be merciful to us.

I first heard the following story thirty-five years ago. Years later, a variation appeared and was made famous by my friend, Tony Orlando, in his song, "Tie a Yellow Ribbon 'Round the Old Oak Tree." I have been told it's a true story, and I believe it, because I believe in the power of mercy.

Three teenagers boarded a bus in New Jersey. Seated on the bus was a quiet, poorly dressed man who sat alone and silent. When the bus made its first stop, everybody got off except this one man, who remained aloof and alone. When the kids came back on the bus, one of them said something nice to him and he smiled shyly.

At the next bus stop, as everybody got off, the last teenager turned and said to the man, "Come on. Get off with us. At least stretch your legs."

So he got off. The teenagers invited him to have lunch with them. One of the young people said, "We are going to Florida for a weekend in the sun. It is nice in Florida, they say."

He said, "Yes, it is."

"Have you been there?"

"Oh, yes," he said, "I used to live there."

One said, "Well, do you still have a home and family?"

He hesitated. "I—I don't know," he said, finally.

"What do you mean, you don't know?" the teenager persisted.

Caught up by their warmth and their sincerity, he shared this story with them:

"Many years ago, I was sentenced to Federal prison. I had a beautiful wife and wonderful children. I said to her, 'Honey, don't write to me. I won't write to you. The kids should not know that their dad is in prison. If you want to, go ahead and find another man—somebody who will be a good father to those boys.'

"I don't know if she kept her part of the bargain. I kept mine. Last week when I knew for sure I was getting out, I wrote a letter to our old address; it's just outside of Jacksonville. I said to her, 'If you are still living there and get this letter, if you haven't found anyone else, and if there is a chance of you taking me back—here is how you can let me know. I will be on the bus as it comes through town. I want you to take a piece of white cloth and hang it in the old oak tree right outside of town.'"

When they got back on the bus and they were about ten miles from Jacksonville, all the teenagers moved to this man's side of the bus and pressed their faces against the windows.

127

Just as they came to the outskirts of Jacksonville there was the big oak tree. The teenagers let out a yell and they jumped out of their seats. They hugged each other and danced in the center of the aisle. All they said was, "Look at it! Look at it!"

Not a single white cloth was tied to the tree. Instead, there was a white bed sheet, a white dress, a little boy's white trousers, and white pillow cases! The whole tree was covered with dozens of pieces of white cloth!

That is the way God treats you and me. It is a promise from God that He will forget the past and erase the record we have rolled up. It is a promise that He will throw away the black pages of our book and give us the kind of big welcome that the Prodigal Son received from his father, who said, "My son that was lost is found and is home again" (Luke 15:24, my paraphrase). This is the *promise* of this Beatitude.

THE POWER PRINCIPLE

The Bible carries a promise—that God will be merciful to us. It also teaches a power principle which appears over and over in the Bible, stated different ways:

- "If you do not forgive men their trespasses, neither will your Father forgive your trespasses" (Matt. 6:15).

- "The measure you give will be the measure you get" (Matt. 7:2).

128

    🍃 "Cast your bread upon the waters, for you will find it after many days" (Eccles. 11:1).

    🍃 "Whatever a man sows, that will he also reap" (Gal. 6:7).

Give a little, you get a little back. Give a lot, you get a lot back. This is the *law of proportionate return* that Jesus is teaching in these verses—and this Beatitude. If you are critical, you can expect people to criticize you. If you gossip about people, you can be sure these same people are going to gossip about you. It is a law of life as real and unavoidable as the physical laws that control our world and our bodies.

Once, when I had laryngitis, I went to my throat doctor. The first thing he did was to get some gauze, wrap it around my tongue, pull my tongue out as far as he could, and stick a flat instrument far back in my throat. Inevitably, I gagged. He did it again. I gagged.

I said, "Done?"

To my dismay he said, "No, I have to do it again. I didn't get to see the vocal cords." Once more he prepared my tongue with another clean piece of gauze.

I said, "This time I'll practice positive thinking and I won't gag."

He said, "Dr. Schuller, that won't work."

"Won't work?" I was appalled! That was the first time anybody had told me that possibility thinking wouldn't work.

The doctor quickly added, "Dr. Schuller, the gag is a reflex. Here, let me show you. Cross your legs." I crossed my legs. He hit my knee. My leg kicked up.

He said, "That's a reflex. The gag is also a reflex. Positive thinking cannot control reflexes, because reflexes come from the spinal cord. They don't pass through the brain."

Let me tell you something. In life there is a principle that you can compare with this biological reflex. If you act a certain way, you will get a certain response; there will be a guaranteed reflex action.

Here is a fundamental rule of life: If you want people to treat you nicely, treat them nicely. For every action, there is a reaction. For every positive action, there is a positive reaction. For every negative action, there is a negative reaction.

If you really want to get high on happiness, look at this Beatitude, and then live it. It really works. *It's impossible to give anything away. Whatever you give away will always come back to you.*

Let me illustrate with a simple object—a seed. It's impossible to throw away seeds. If you throw them on the ground, they sprout and grow.

As many of you know, I was born on an Iowa farm. Adjoining my family's farm was a river, which thrilled me because I loved to fish. I remember one time when a city kid came for a few weeks to visit the neighbors across the road. The city kid was our neighbor's nephew. His uncle had welcomed him but warned that he would have to help out with the work.

One day the city kid's Uncle John gave his nephew a can of beans to plant. He explained, "Just dig a little hole, put in a couple of beans, and stomp the dirt down on top of them. Do it all the way along the fence until you get to the end."

Unaware of the task that had been assigned to this city lad, I invited him to join me fishing. He replied, "Uncle John said I have to plant these beans. He said that I have to dig a little hole, put in three beans, and stomp it down."

I said, "Oh, that's too bad; I wish you could go fishing with me. Ever been fishing?"

"No, I'd like to go fishing with you, but I've got to finish these beans." From the looks of the full can, it appeared that he'd just started. Directly in front of him was a stump. Suddenly he had an idea! "Uncle John will never know," he said, as he dug a hole, dumped in all the beans, and covered them with dirt. He turned away from his task and said, "Let's go fishing!"

We had a grand time, and we caught a good number of fish. Coming home with all our catch, we ran into Uncle John.

He said "I see you've been fishin' …. did you get all the beans planted?"

His nephew said, "Sure did, Uncle John."

"That's great. Glad to hear it. And you still had time to fish?"

"M-m-m-, yeah."

"I'm surprised you were able to plant them so quickly."

He answered, "I work fast."

Uncle John seemed to accept his word for it. Soon it was time for the boy to return home. Months passed. The summer was drawing to a close. The city kid returned for a last visit before school started.

Uncle John said to him, "Hey, would you like to see those beans you planted?" They walked out behind the farmhouse. There was a neat row of beans for about fifty feet. Suddenly there was a stump of a tree covered with uncontrolled vines!

You can't fool nature, and you can't play with God. You can't tamper with natural laws. And this is a natural law: *If you treat people nicely, you will probably be treated nicely. The kinder you are to others, the more kindness you are likely to receive in life.* It is the law of proportionate return, and there's no way of getting around it.

THE PRESCRIPTION

The *prescription* for joyful living is very simple: If you want to be happy, treat people right. If you carry somebody else's burdens, in the process you'll discover the secret of happiness.

Everybody wants to be happy. I've observed in the world today that there are those who are trying to reach happiness with selfishness, yet these people end up in a hell on earth. There are others who try to obtain joy by following the laws of Christ, by helping somebody else. If you live by the laws

*God's care
will carry
you so
you can
carry others!*

of Christ and choose to look for people who have burdens, you might be able to help them. But if you look for your own happiness, ignoring the needs of those around you, you will lose out altogether.

There is a story of a man who had a dream one night. He dreamed that he died and found himself immediately in a large room. In the room there was a huge banquet table filled with all sorts of delicious food. Around the banquet table were people seated on chairs, obviously hungry. But the chairs were five feet from the edge of the table and the people apparently could not get out of the chairs. Furthermore, their arms were not long enough to reach the food on the table.

In the dream there was one single large spoon, five feet long. Everyone was fighting, quarreling, pushing each other, trying to grab hold of that spoon. Finally, in an awful scene, one strong bully got hold of the spoon. He reached out, picked up some food, and turned it to feed himself, only to find that the spoon was so long that as he held it out he could not touch his mouth. The food fell off. Immediately, someone else grabbed the spoon. Again, the person reached far enough to pick up the food, but he could not feed himself. The handle was too long.

In the dream, the man who was observing it all said to his guide, "This is hell—to have food and not be able to eat it."

The guide replied, "Where do you think you are? This is hell. But this is not your place. Come with me."

And they went into another room. In this room there was also a long table filled with food, exactly as in the other room. Everyone was seated in chairs, and for some reason they, too, seemed unable to get out of their chairs.

Like the others, they were unable to reach the food on the table. Yet they had a satisfied, pleasant look on their faces. Only then did the visitor see the reason why. Exactly as before, there was only one spoon. It, too, had a handle five feet long. Yet no one was fighting for it. In fact, one man, who held the handle, reached out, picked up the food, and put it into the mouth of someone else, who ate it and was satisfied.

That person then took the spoon by the handle, reached for the food from the table, and put it back to the mouth of the man who had just given him something to eat. And the guide said, "This is heaven."

"Blessed are the merciful, for they shall obtain mercy."

Another Bible verse says it in another way, "Bear one another's burdens, and so fulfill the law of Christ" (Gal. 6:2).

It is impossible to have thoughts of resentment and jealousy, anger and hate and ill-will—and be happy. You cannot sow these negative emotional seeds and expect to raise a harvest of smiles and laughter. Nobody can be happy and bitter at the same time. It is so incredibly simple.

The secret to the prescription then is to care. Caring becomes carrying.

I am sure you have heard of Mother Teresa of Calcutta. She's been listed frequently in *Good Housekeeping* magazine's most-admired-women list. She is one of the most beautiful persons alive in the world today.

You probably know that Mother Teresa is about sixty years old and that she is an amazing person. But let me tell you more about her. Mother Teresa was the child of a peasant family in Yugoslavia. She was taken regularly to church, where she met Jesus Christ. As a teenager she felt a calling to go into full-time church work, and she became a Catholic sister. One day a missionary spoke to her home congregation about the great need to bring Christ to the people in India, so Teresa volunteered and was accepted for a teaching post in Calcutta.

At the convent in Calcutta, Teresa enjoyed very lovely quarters. She had beautiful accommodations that were surrounded by lovely gardens. She did her teaching in a very lovely and attractive classroom. But one day she had to make a trip to the dirtiest part of the town. When she walked the streets alone, through the back parts of Calcutta, she saw something she had never seen before. She saw human beings dying, and nobody was paying any attention to them. When she inquired, she found that this was very common. Nobody had time for the dying; there was no place for them to go. The young nun was haunted by this terrible situation. She felt that Jesus Christ was saying to her, "I am going to call you to serve the poorest of the poor. I am calling you to minister not to the living, but to the dying."

This was such a strong call that she asked the Church to

release her from her vows. It took two years, but finally she was released. No longer a nun, she was sent out of the convent and into the streets of Calcutta. With only a few rupees, or pennies, in her pocket, she shuffled down the streets with no promise of a meal and no promise of clothing from the church. She was on her own, and she prayed, "Jesus, lead me to somebody who is dying all alone."

Two blocks away she saw an old lady lying in the gutter on the main street. The living body was being eaten by the rats that were running in the gutter. She picked up the woman and literally dragged her to the nearest hospital. She was refused admittance. "But," she exclaimed, "this woman is dying." She was told, "People die in the streets of Calcutta all the time. We cannot take her." Teresa refused to leave until they had taken the dying woman. She said, "If there is a God in heaven, and a Christ we love, nobody should die alone."

Shortly thereafter Teresa went to the city government and asked for an empty room—"a place where I can build a home for the dying." The civil authorities told her, "Well, we have this empty Hindu temple of Kali, if that would suit you." She said, "Beautiful. It would be beautiful for God. That is all I want to do in my life—something beautiful for God."

Two other sisters heard about Teresa's project, and they helped to drag the dying from the streets into this Hindu temple. Without medicine, without money, without an organization, without any backing, they did what they could, and nobody died in their place without at least a touch on the cheek and a kind word: "We love you." "Go in peace with God." They did not die alone.

Today, Teresa—or Mother Teresa, as she is widely known—is probably the closest thing to an authentic saint living on planet earth. She has created her own Sisterhood called the Sisters of Charity. It is a pontificate, which means it is now recognized directly below the Pope who, when he came to Calcutta to see what this strange ex-nun was doing, was so impressed that he gave her as a gift his own private, expensive white limousine. She took one look at this big, expensive car and said, "Oh, thank you."

The first thing she did was to announce a raffle. The money went for her house for the dying. Today, she has over ten thousand dying lepers in her colony. Her colonies have spread into twenty-eight cities, to Ceylon, to the Indian people who live in London, Rome, Venezuela, and Australia. She and all of those who are members of the Missionaries of Charity have taken the vow of total poverty. The only thing they may own is the cheapest cotton garment and a pair of sandals. Total surrender!

Malcolm Muggeridge, who interviewed Mother Teresa on the British Broadcasting Company and later visited her in Calcutta, said, "The thing I noticed about you and the hundreds of sisters who now form your team is that you all look so happy. Is it a put-on?" She said, "Oh no, not at all. Nothing makes you happier than when you really reach out in mercy to someone who is badly hurt."

"Blessed are the merciful, for they shall obtain mercy."

Service is its own reward. A prescription for joyful living is: "Be good, be kind, be unselfish. Do unto others as you would have them do unto you."

If you want positive things to happen, you must be positive. If you want to be friendly with people and if you want people to be friendly toward you, be friendly to them. If you are surrounded by undesirable people, change them into good people.

How do you change them into good people? Bring the best out of them! How do you bring the best out of them? Call attention to the best that is within them! Until they begin to believe they are beautiful people, they will not treat you beautifully.

I'll never forget the young wife who came to see me. She complained, "My husband never compliments me. All he does is criticize! It doesn't matter what I do, how hard I work; I only hear how I could have done it better!"

I suggested, "You know that people who are highly critical often suffer from a low self-esteem. Is it possible that your husband has trouble in that regard?"

She thought for a moment. "Yes, I think that's possible."

"Well," I replied, "then it seems to me that the way to help him with his self-esteem and his critical remarks is for you to start complimenting him!"

"Oh! I never thought of that!" she cried. "But you're right! I can't remember the last time I complimented him.

I've been so busy looking for compliments *from* him that I've completely neglected compliments *for* him."

If you want to change your world, change yourself. How do you change yourself? How do you become this kind of positive-thinking person? I know only one way. Education does not do it. Legislation does not do it. However, there is a living God—and a living Christ—who does. Christ can come into hearts that are filled with fear, anger, bitterness, and hurt, and He can liberate them with His mercy. It can happen to you. It happens when you meet Jesus Christ and ask Him to take over your life.

If you want to treat people mercifully, you have to begin by treating yourself mercifully. Accept yourself by knowing that Christ accepts you just as you are! However, if you lack a deep inner sense of self-esteem and self-worth, you will constantly have problems with other people. You won't treat them mercifully. You'll be unkind. You'll be critical or you'll gossip. You'll lash back until you've undermined the most important aspects of your life—and you find it collapsed around you.

Think about it. What is it that keeps us from treating people mercifully? It's resentment, jealousy, or the feeling that someone is a threat to you. If you can't handle resentment, jealousy, or "victimitis," then deep down in your own mind, heart, and soul you need to deal with your lack of a positive self-image. Your negative reactions are the result of hidden wounds that need to be healed.

*Selfishness
turns
life into
a burden.
Unselfishness
turns
burdens
into life!*

HEALING FOR THE HIDDEN WOUND

Do you have trouble with this Be-Happy Attitude? Do you have trouble being merciful? Are you critical of yourself as well as of others? If so, then you need to identify, isolate, and heal your hidden wounds. The first step toward healing is to realize that you are not alone. Everyone has been wounded at some time or another. Even Jesus, the Son of God, had wounds. Stop and count them; there were six:

(1) The ankles, where the nail went through.

(2) The palms of the hands, which were also pierced by nails.

(3) The brow, which was bloodied by the crown of thorns.

(4) The side, which was slashed by a spear.

(5) The back, which bore the stripes of a lashing.

Those are five of Christ's wounds. But the sixth wound was the hidden wound:

(6) The wound in His heart, placed there by the kiss of one of His own disciples. The hidden wound was the most painful of them all.

We all have them, don't we? We may disguise our wounds behind a smile and keep our guard up. But if we really searched our lives, exposed ourselves, we would find that every person has a secret pain, an intimate agony, a private hurt—a very isolated, unrevealed, unexposed wound.

Society inflicts hidden wounds on us. Some of you have been the victims of racial or ethnic prejudice, or of some other form of painful discrimination such as sexism or ageism. You know the discomfort of being laughed at, ignored, not being allowed to fulfill your vocational dreams, just because you are a certain race, sex, or age.

Sometimes those people closest to us inflict the deepest, most painful wounds. Some of you would weep right now, if I touched the tender memory, because of what a father or a mother, a spouse, child, lover, employer, or friend did to you.

Other hidden wounds we inflict on ourselves. We react too negatively to circumstances; we wound ourselves because we take them much too seriously. We read too much into other people's actions and exaggerate their rejection of us.

The hidden wounds you carry with you today—those private hurts that you can't talk about—what were the weapons that inflicted them on your heart? Look at the wounds of Jesus. The external wounds were inflicted by nails, a crown of thorns, a spear, a lash. But His hidden wound was caused by a kiss.

The weapons that wounded you are probably just as common as a kiss. They are words, looks, body language.

Someone turned his or her back on you, didn't return your gesture of love and friendship, and that hurt. You were received with silence; maybe it was a snub. You were passed over. You never got the invitation. You were rebuffed. Words, looks, actions—these are the horrible weapons that inflict hidden wounds in human hearts.

Now the question is, *What do we do with these hidden wounds? How do we handle them?*

First of all, *don't nurse them.* There are many people who delight in nursing their hidden wounds. They still remember how their mother treated them. How their father treated them. How their first husband or first wife treated them. Thirty years later they are still obsessed with the wound. This is a neurotic, negative reaction.

Don't curse them. Don't let your wounds make you a bitter person. Don't allow anger at God or at the person who hurt you so deeply control your life. Don't curse your hurts, and *don't rehearse them.* Try to forget them. Remember, you can't forget your hurts if you keep talking about them *all the time.* One of the great men on the staff of the church for thirty years here was a minister named Dr. Henry Poppen. Dr. Henry Poppen had been a missionary in China and was held prisoner for many months in a little town in China when the Communists took over. He was kept in solitary confinement, and the treatment he received was abysmal. The experience was tragic. It was horrific. It was awful. He escaped by a miracle; most of the other missionaries were killed on sight.

Well, when he came out he was an emotionally wounded man. But he found healing for that wound through a doctor who said, "Don't talk about it any more. Just forget it." In Dr. Poppen's case, these words of advice were just what he needed. His memories were so ugly that to have shared them over and over would have only made them that much more a part of his life.

Don't nurse the wound. Don't curse the wound. Don't keep rehearsing the wounding experience. What do you do with your hidden wounds? Immerse them. Drown them in a life of noble service.

I remember a time in the early years of my ministry when I had a real personal problem with someone. Sometimes it hurt me so badly I didn't know how to handle it. At these times my wife always had a solution. She'd say, "I think you should go out and call on Rosie Gray." Or "I think you ought to visit Marie; it was a year ago that her husband died."

So I would go out to the hospitals and I would go calling on people. I would immerse myself as a pastor in the hearts of people who were hurting. And in the process, my little hidden wound was just drowned to death. It up and died.

How do you handle your hidden wounds? Don't nurse them. Don't curse them. Don't rehearse them. Do immerse them. And finally, reverse them. Turn the negative into a positive. You do that when you allow your wound to turn you into a more sensitive, compassionate, considerate, thoughtful, merciful, gracious person.

If your wound is something that you can't share with others without criticizing somebody else or tearing him or her down, then you have to suffer in silence. If that's the case, then trust God. Let Him heal your hidden wounds.

She is no longer with us—our dear Schug. Her name was Bernice Schug, but my children called her simply "Schug." Since both my wife's and my families lived in the Midwest, our children were unable to spend much time with their grandparents.

When we met Schug at church she was a widow. Her own grandchildren lived in northern California, so she was unable to see them as often as she liked. It was inevitable then that Schug would become our California grandmother. She lavished love and poppy-seed rolls on us and our children. She stayed over with the children when my wife had our last two children. She ate meals with us, she cared for our children, yet none of us knew how deep her hidden wound was.

One day Schug came to me and said, "Bob, I was reading in the church bulletin today that you are having a guest speaker next Sunday. I see you're having a Kamikaze pilot as your guest."

Oh! I remembered then that Schug's son had been killed in World War II by a Kamikaze pilot. "That's right, Schug. This particular pilot was trained as a Kamikaze and would have died as a Kamikaze had the war not ended when it did. But he has a tremendous story to tell of how he found Jesus."

"That may be. I don't think I will be in church that Sunday, though. I don't think I could handle it."

"I understand," I replied. "I don't think it will hurt if you miss one Sunday."

The next Sunday the Japanese pilot shared his story. His love and gratitude for Jesus shone from his black eyes. You could feel the love and release he had found. People were moved by his testimony. And when the service was over, my associate pastor walked with him back down the aisle to the rear of the church.

Suddenly as they approached the last pew, an older woman stepped out. She stood firmly in front of the Kamikaze pilot and blocked his exit. She looked at him squarely and said, "My son was killed in the war by a Kamikaze!"

It was Schug. We all held our breath as she continued, "God has forgiven you for your sins, and tonight He has forgiven me of mine."

She threw her arms around this little Japanese pilot and hugged him and cried and cried as she released all the bitterness and anger that had been harbored for so many years.

Forgive a Kamikaze pilot, when a fellow pilot had killed a beloved son? Impossible! Yes, it is impossible for us, but not impossible for God!

After all, who is a better teacher on the subject of forgiveness than Jesus Christ? When He hung on the cross, brutally whipped, mocked with a crown of thorns, betrayed by His friend, and deserted by His disciples, what did He say to the people who watched Him die?

He said, *"Forgive them; for they know not what they do"* (Luke 23:34).

Jesus is an expert on forgiveness. Let Him forgive you and heal you of your hidden wounds.

If you are merciful, people will treat you mercifully. If you are merciful, then God will release you from vengeful attitudes that will eat at you and destroy you. When you follow the example that Christ set, you will find, much to your surprise, that God will step in and bless you, too, with an Easter morning!

"I'VE GOT TO LET THE FAITH FLOW FREE THROUGH ME."

Blessed are the pure in heart, for they shall see God.

DO YOU LONG TO know God better? Do you struggle with doubt? Do you ever wish you had more faith?

If so, you are not alone.

I have been in the ministry long enough to know that even people who have been Christians all their lives have to deal with doubt at one time or another. Many committed Christians go through "dry" times when God seems absent or far away. And there are countless people inside and outside the church—even some who claim to be agnostic or even atheist—who really *want* to believe, but who somehow have trouble developing a strong faith. If this is your struggle—to have more faith, to conquer doubt, to know God in a real, personal, life-changing way—then this Be-Happy Attitude is for you: "Blessed are the pure in heart," Jesus said, "for they shall see God."

But what does it take to become "pure in heart"? I would like to suggest four steps that can really help: (1) Wise up. (2) Clean up. (3) Give up. (4) Take up.

WISE UP!

If you could collect the smartest intellectuals from around the world, bring them together, and ask them one question, "How many of you believe in God?" several hands would go up. On the other hand, many hands would go up if you asked, "How many of you do not believe in God?"

If you divide the smartest, most educated minds of the world into believers and unbelievers, there would be quite a few in each group. That is because faith in God is not a matter of intelligence. Faith is not a result of intellect, any more than it is a result of ignorance.

Faith is not a matter of intelligence. It is a matter of instinct. Even science has recently confirmed the power of innate, inbred instinct. A notable example is the recent experiment by Dr. Maurice, a scholar and a student of the weaver bird of South Africa. This interesting little bird makes its nest out of reeds, lines it with silky grass, and does what no other bird does—he makes a hole in the bottom of his nest through which he makes his entrance.

Dr. Maurice, trying to test the strength of instinctive drives, took two eggs from a nest in South Africa, transported them out of the country, and incubated them until they hatched. He successfully raised the birds in cages through four and even five generations. None of these birds ever had any exposure to nests with a hole in the bottom of it.

Dr. Maurice took the fifth generation of weaver birds, brought them back to South Africa, and released them in their natural habitat. The birds found reeds, immediately lined their nests with silky grass, and then made holes in the bottom. Incredible!

There are mysteries in anthropology and natural science—mysteries that can only be described as instinctive. These instincts are powerful; they can propel swarms of bees, herds of whales, schools of salmon, flocks of geese thousands of miles. These instincts are also enduring; animals who are born with their peculiar instinctive modes of behavior have them as long as their species is in its native habitat.

Someone once said, "When God wants to make sure a truth is never abandoned or aborted, He will put it in the instinct." When God wanted to ensure that the need for religion would never die, He put it within the human breast. That is why humankind throughout history has been drawn to a belief in a God. Even the aborigines of Australia and the headhunters in New Guinea believe in a god or gods. They feel the instinctive urge within their souls to know and worship something greater than themselves.

Instinct. How else do you explain Bill Murray, son of the militant atheist, Madelyn Murray O'Hare? He was raised and indoctrinated in atheism, and he worked with his mother for years, but he still had a life-transforming experience that turned him into a believer in God.

If you are struggling with the idea of faith, wise up! Realize that God has planted faith within the instinct of every healthy human being. Just as a healthy bird instinctively takes to the trees, just as a healthy fish swims in the water, so the healthy human being is inclined to be religious. However, just as animals lose some of their innate drives when taken from their natural habitats, so man loses his innate ability to believe in a loving God when he is away too long from positive, faith-producing environments. That is why it is so important to carefully surround ourselves with positive, believing, healthy people.

Religion is a sign of health. Skepticism is a mark of illness. Unbelief is abnormal; belief is normal. For the normal human being will joyfully embrace faith and belief, but the cynical doubter cannot believe and will not believe until he can be healed of the negative memories that plague him and block him from his innate ability to see God.

Dr. Gerald Jampolsky, a noted psychiatrist and a dear

friend of mine, was for twenty-five years a very strong agnostic. Then one day, without warning, his life totally changed, and he became a believer in God. I asked him once when we were together, "Dr. Jampolsky, in the years before you were converted, what did you think about people who went to church?"

He said, "For twenty-five years I thought people who went to church, prayed, and believed in God were not normal. I thought they were really kind of sick. Now I see that I was completely wrong. *They* were normal; I was not."

CLEAN UP!

If the first step toward developing more faith is to wise up—to realize that belief is instinctive, normal, and healthy—then the second step is to clean up any negative emotions in your life that might be blocking your faith and keeping you from "seeing" God.

There was a time when my children were little that I was going through some torturing times with the development of my church. I had colossal burdens and pressures. And although I was going through the motions of being a pastor, a husband, and a father, my heart was not really in any of these. It was blocked by despair, depression, and fear.

Often during this time I would come home from the office, sit in a chair, pick up the paper, and read column after column without really being aware of anything I had read.

My little boy would come and talk to me, and I'd respond, "Yes, Bobbie." But I wouldn't really hear him.

One day my wife and I were walking through the garden. I remarked, "Honey, the roses are blooming." To my surprise, she replied, "They've been blooming for three months."

It was not until I cried out to God and asked Him to release me from my anxieties and worries that I was able once more to feel His presence. Like a finger pressing into my brain, He touched me, and I felt the fear and the despair drain out of me. In its place flowed peace, joy, and hope, despite the obstacles that still lay ahead.

When God touched me, my ears were opened. I could once again hear what my family was saying to me. My eyes were opened. I could once again see the beauty that God had created. I could even see possible solutions for the overwhelming problems I was facing.

Worry, anxiety, pressures, frustrations—all of these can cause us to be blinded to the real world all around us. When we take this one step further, you can see how easy it would be for some emotional blockage to keep us from being aware of the presence of God.

"Blessed are the pure in heart, for they shall see God." I believe Jesus is teaching that if we have emotional and spiritual health we will be able to "see" God, to believe in Him.

Dear Dr. Schuller:

I must write to tell you—when you spoke of

the seed of grass that had been tossed from a vase and wedged uncomfortably in a crack in the sidewalk, to be trampled under the boots of men— well, that was my life, my early childhood.

My parents were well bred. Money and fame was their God. But I was never able to trust their love. Consequently, I was never able to believe in a loving father. However, I became aware that Christians were happy. I was not. I knew that my personality was disjointed and disconnected.

One day, after hearing your sermon when you said to put God first, others second, and yourself third, I offered God everything I had. I offered Him my money, my time, myself. I said, "God, I'm willing to be Yours if You'll help me."

The following Thursday happened to be Maundy Thursday. I noticed a little church with a sign saying, "Communion Today." I went in. I took the communion and, as I did, I asked God to make me into a mentally healthy person so that I would be able to be a believer. At that moment, it all happened. I felt cleansed of all the evil I had carried with me since childhood. I cannot tell you how happy and relieved I feel.

Then the writer of this letter added this very perceptive and analytically profound postscript: "P.S. It is a tremendous

"In the presence
of hope,
faith is born.

In the presence
of faith, love
becomes a possibility!

In the presence of love,
miracles happen!"

achievement for the emotionally disturbed person to trust God!"

How right she is! It is a difficult task for a person who has emotional difficulties to become a healthy believer in God. And so I ask you:

- Is it possible that somewhere in your subconscious there lurks hostility toward your father or your mother?

- Is it possible that you have within your subconscious some negative feeling toward your family, your friends, your business associates or competitors?

- Have you ever been hurt by someone who never came back to apologize to you?

- Do you have a secret that you have never shared with any other living human being—about something you have done, are doing, or are thinking about doing, which is either illegal or immoral?

- Have you suffered grief and heartache, and did your prayers seem unanswered?

- Do you feel inferior to others, and do you have trouble loving yourself?

There are countless questions I could ask. Let me just say that if you answered "yes" to any one of these questions, you are not totally free of negative emotions. And as long as you have negative emotions within yourself, then listen carefully: *Don't trust your doubt.* Doubt is a subconscious defense mechanism fabricated by an insecure, guilty, or troubled mind to keep us from believing in a God who might make demands upon us we're not prepared to meet.

Negative emotions block faith because they hinder us from confronting our need for God. It's like the overweight person who won't step on the bathroom scale or the person with overdue bills who won't look in the mailbox. When we most need help, negative emotions can keep us from turning to the One who could help us most; they block us from believing and seeing God's plan for our lives.

Now you know why Jesus was such a powerful believer! Jesus knew God. Jesus Christ had no emotional blockages! He had no selfish ambitions, no greed, no jealousies, no hatred, no self-pity, no selfish griefs. Emotionally, He was constantly positive. He was "pure in heart."

So if there is within your personality some resentment, some hostility, some guilt, some fear or worry, find it. Get rid of it. You will be surprised to find how much your faith will improve. How natural it will seem to you to be religious—as natural and normal as breathing.

I love a story I once heard about Leonardo da Vinci. According to the legend, some lads were visiting the famous artist. One of them knocked over a stack of canvases. This upset the artist because he was working very quietly and sensitively. He became angry, threw his brush, and hurled some harsh words to the hapless little fellow, who ran crying from the studio.

The artist was now alone again, and he tried to continue his work. He was trying to paint the face of Jesus, but he couldn't do it. His creativity had stopped.

Leonardo da Vinci put down his brush. He went out and walked the streets and the alleys until he found the little boy. He said, "I'm sorry, son; I shouldn't have spoken so harshly. Forgive me, even as Christ forgives. I have done something worse than you. You only knocked over the canvases. But I, by my anger, blocked the flow of God into my life. Will you come back with me?"

He took the boy back into the studio with him. They smiled as the face of Jesus came quite naturally from the master's brush. That face has been an inspiration to millions ever since.

If there is a negative emotion within you that is blocking you in your relationship with God, *clean up!* "Blessed are the pure in heart, for they shall see God." Here are some exercises to help you:

(1) Think of some hidden hurt in your past and pray a forgiving prayer for the person who was the cause of your hurt. C. S. Lewis said it: "We all agree that forgiveness is a beautiful idea until we have to practice it!"

(2) Think of someone of whom you are jealous, and pray for that person's continued prosperity.

(3) Think of someone you've hurt, cheated, insulted, slighted, snubbed, or criticized. Call him or her. Invite this person to have dinner or lunch with you. Confess to him or her your Un-Christian attitude, and ask for forgiveness.

(4) Think of some neglected cause, project, or person. Surprise yourself with a streak of generosity! Really give a lot—of yourself and of your substance.

(5) Pray a totally honest prayer to Christ. You doubt God? Tell Him so. He'll still love you, even if you don't believe in Him! (God specializes in loving sinners!)

Perhaps you read the amazing story of the young Air Force man who is alive today because of the complete change of blood in his body. He had hepatitis and his liver was nearly useless. Doctors drained every cell of blood from this man's body and substituted a saline solution. They lowered his body temperature to eighty-five degrees. For eight or ten minutes he was, for all practical purposes, physically dead. The doctors then flushed the saline solution out and filled his veins and arteries with new, healthy blood. A medical miracle had occurred—a human life had been saved. Amazing!

Jesus said that if you want to see God, you have to be born again. Another way of saying this is that you need a spiritual "blood" transfusion. The old negative blood is drawn out. Then the new spirit of Jesus Christ, like new blood, flows through your entire nervous and emotional system, and you become a new person! "If any man is in Christ, he is a new creature." Through the Holy Spirit, you receive "new spiritual blood" in every cell. If doctors could give new life to an Air Force man, just imagine what God could do inside your mind!

Do you want a life-changing experience with God? Clean up—wash your mistakes away through Christ's grace. Accept the forgiveness of Jesus. Let Him clear up the negative, emotional blockages.

GIVE UP!

Do you want a life-changing experience with God? If so, wise up! Realize it's instinctive and normal to be religious. Clean up! Wash your mistakes and negative emotions away through Christ's grace. And the third step is: Give up—anything that may be hindering you. Perhaps there is something in your life that you will have to relinquish, with God's help. If it is something that is blocking the birth of real faith, then you may have to give it up. If it is a choice between living and a bad habit—choose life.

Many years ago I officiated in the marriage ceremony of a Hollywood actor, Glenn Ford. Waiting for the ceremony to begin, we chatted in a back room of his home. Gathered in that room were Glenn Ford; his best man, Bill Holden; Frank Sinatra; Jimmy Stewart; and John Wayne.

"You know, you should quit smoking, Francis," John Wayne said to Sinatra, who smiled.

Before he could answer, Jimmy Stewart asked Wayne, "When did you give up smoking, Duke?"

I'll never forget his answer: "When I decided it was more important to live than to smoke."

We can find the strength to give something up when it threatens something that is precious to us—such as life.

Dr. Kenneth Cooper, best-selling author and founder of a world-famous fitness center in Dallas, Texas, is an authority on health and fitness, the man who first made *aerobics* a household word. In my opinion, Dr. Cooper is responsible more than any other single person for contributing to the physical fitness movement that is going on in the United States and around the world. Several years ago I interviewed him on *The Hour of Power,* and before my national television audience the following dialogue took place concerning negative habits and how to give them up:

K.C.: "There are at least fifty million overweight Americans with a total of one billion pounds above their ideal weight. I hope we don't sink off the face of the earth with statistics like that. It was an indictment of an overweight society when they renovated Yankee Stadium a few years ago. They had to reduce the seating capacity by nine thousand seats, because they couldn't change the overall dimensions of the stadium but they had to increase the width of each seat from nineteen to twenty-two inches—to accommodate the modern American's posterior! We have a lot of obesity in America.

R.S.: "So, are you saying that we need to exercise and cut back on our eating?"

K.C.: "Absolutely. Obesity is rampant in our country, and obesity is accompanied by everything from high blood pressure to diabetes to heart disease and even depression."

R.S.: [I felt that I had to toot my own horn just a little.] "You know, a few years ago I cut out white bread, cookies, and sugar. I only take fresh fruit for dessert."

K.C.: "Bob, without question, you're doing yourself a lot of good. We recommend restricting cholesterol, cutting down on sweets, and concentrating on natural foods—on fresh vegetables, fruit, and lean meat. That's what we as American people need to do. In our Aerobics Center we encourage people to check with their physician first, to have their blood analyzed to find out what their cholesterol level is, what their triglycerides are, what their fasting blood sugar level is. From that they can be given specific guidelines as to what they should do to change their diets to improve their statistics."

R.S.: "You also have strong feelings about tobacco and smoking?"

K.C.: "Most definitely! The worst health hazard that we have in America today is cigarette smoking. Let me cite some quick statistics: If you smoke more than one pack of cigarettes a day, you're three times more likely to die of a heart attack than the nonsmoker or the former cigarette smoker. But the exciting thing is that when the cigarette smokers stop smoking, in as short a period of time as six months he or she can drop back into the low-risk category for heart disease. That's why I strongly believe that the dramatic improvement in the health of our people in the past fifteen to twenty years has been due to the fact that thirty million have quit smoking cigarettes since 1964."

R.S.: "Cigarettes are, as they say, 'nails in the coffin'?"

K.C.: "They really are. And remember, too, recent studies show that for every cigarette you smoke, you increase the likelihood of lung cancer by that much. For example, if you smoke *five* cigarettes a day, you are *five* times more likely to die of lung cancer. If you smoke *thirty* cigarettes a day, you're thirty times more likely to die of lung cancer than the non-smoker. The statistics just go up and up."

R.S.: "But how can people give up smoking? How can they lose weight?"

K.C.: "I recommend first of all that they start an exercise program. For some reason, that gives them a discipline they didn't have before. All is possible through God. Some will be successful on their own, but many others will succeed only when they ask for God's help."

"Blessed are the pure in heart." It is always wise to give up anything that you think might be blocking you from a clear relationship with God.

I witness to you that the times I felt closest to God were the times when I gave up something I desired very much. My experience proves the words of our Lord, who said, "If any man would come after me, let him deny himself and take up the cross and follow me."

Recently, with my doctor's enthusiastic approval, I went on a fast. For six days I had no solid foods. During this time, I sometimes felt hungry, but I also felt especially close to Jesus Christ.

I remember the first time I began tithing, giving God ten percent of my earnings. Boy, was it tough. I had to give up something, but I did feel closer to God.

Years ago, I smoked. You must understand that there were no cultural biases against smoking in the community where I grew up. In my childhood church, all good Dutch preachers smoked cigars or pipes. However, I became convinced that, for me, smoking was not right, and I gave the habit up. It was difficult, but once I had quit, I felt great.

You see, fasting and tithing and giving up smoking were

all part of the principle of doing something difficult with God's help and making it a success. It was an adventure of walking by faith which gave God a chance to prove Himself to me. And He did!

Now, please understand that I am not saying you have to quit smoking or lose weight before you can "see God." But I am suggesting that becoming "pure in heart" may mean you have to give up something you like very much. It may be money. It may be smoking. It may be overeating. It may be alcohol or other habit-forming drugs. It may be extramarital sex. I do not know what it is that is blocking you from a close relationship with God. I don't *want* to know what it is; that is between you and Him. But make it a spiritual adventure and you will have an experience with God. Many people have a low faith level simply because they are scared to stick their necks out with God. Try it!

TAKE UP!

Dr. Cooper suggested taking up an exercise program as the first step on the road to better health. The same principle applies to our spiritual walk. To be pure in heart, we need to take up something:

🎵 a dream . . .

🎵 a project . . .

🎵 God's call to do something great!

166

*You can
live
without
something*

—

*if you have
someone
to live for!*

After all, what does "pure in heart" mean? Does it mean that we are sinless? Of course not. If that's what it meant, Jesus would have been giving all of us an assignment that was doomed to fail. I'm not sinless. You are not sinless. None of us is entirely sinless.

If Jesus is not requiring us to be sinless, then, what *does* He mean when He says, "Blessed are the pure in heart"?

As I mentioned in an earlier chapter, a *pure* field is not one that has merely been plowed so that it's free of weeds. No, a pure field is a productive one—where corn, pineapples, or oranges are being grown.

The same is true in our lives. We can believe in God, we can see Him, we can catch His vision for our lives, we can feel His spirit moving in our lives when we:

   🐾 wise up,

     🐾 clean up,

       🐾 give up, and finally,

         🐾 take up God's call to do something great for Him.

There is one consuming cause that I can offer you—the cause of Christ in our world today. God is alive, and Christ is alive, and there are millions who are finding Him. If you have not found Him, you have the greatest experience of your life still coming! I offer to you Jesus Christ as your cause.

Take up a "cause," and it's easy to give up "things."

A young married couple living in a cheap little apartment are happy. Why? Because they have a cause—their new married love.

An artist lives in a musty attic ill-fed, ill-clothed. But he is happy! Why? Because he has a cause to live for . . . his art. He does not need many material things.

A research scientist who comes to his classroom in baggy pants, with an unshaven face and no tie, isn't interested in expensive suits. He is lost in a cause—that of research and study.

You can get by without a lot of things if you have something great to live for. Jesus said, "Seek first his kingdom and his righteousness, and all these things shall be added unto you" (Matt. 6:33).

Do you want to have a real experience with God? Wise up. Clean up. Give up. And take up the cross of Jesus Christ. God is offering to you a cause—Christ's cause. Jesus needs you.

> *Christ has no hands but our hands to do His work today.*
> *He has no feet, but our feet to lead men on the way.*
> *He has no tongues but our tongues to tell men how He died.*
> *He has no help but our help to draw men to His side.*

It is that simple. Have you given your heart to Him? Maybe you are a Christian and have accepted Christ, but God is not real enough to you. Maybe there is something in your heart that needs cleansing. Maybe you have to give up something, or take up something.

I told you in the previous chapter about Mother Teresa. Mother Teresa left the shelter and the security of the convent with only a few rupees in her pocket. She went out into the poorest section in the vast city of Calcutta. She found a woman being eaten by rats while still alive, and she dragged this woman to a hospital. That is how she began her life work. Today, she is dedicated to helping the poorest of the poor. Those who have met her say she has a radiant, God-filled face. No wonder . . . listen to her!

She writes: "Joy. Joy is prayer. Joy is strength. Joy is love. God loves a cheerful giver. She gives most who gives joy. The best way to show my gratitude to God is to accept everything, even my problems, with joy. A joyful heart is a normal result of a heart that is burning with love. Never let anything so fill you with sorrow as to make you forget for one moment the joy of Christ risen."

She goes on: "We all long for heaven, where God is. But we have it in our power to be in heaven with God right now, at this very moment. But to be at home with God now means loving the unlovely as He does, helping the helpless as He does, giving to those in need as He gives, serving the lonely as He serves, rescuing the perishing as He rescues. This is my Christ. This is the way I live."

God is so real. He will be real to you, too, if you take Christ into your heart. Adopt Mother Teresa's goal to "do something beautiful for God." Look around you now to help someone who is hurting. Do it for Christ's sake.

If you want a life-changing experience with God, a dynamic faith, here's how you can get it. Ask God to take your life, to heal the subconscious memories. Ask Jesus Christ to forgive you for your secret sins. Then ask Him to take your life and show you how you can be a part of something beautiful for God! For faith combined with good works makes God come alive within you.

Take a look at a fountain pen. The ink flows through it to form words—communication. If you simply give your life to Him today, He can flow through you. He can make your heart right. He can clear the rubbish from your life and replace it with a holy dream! And you'll come to realize that the burning desire, the consuming dream, the strong sense of destiny—yes, all of this inner drive—is the very life of God surging in your soul! Your dream is God within you!

It is a decision! To become a believer! And decide that a positive mental attitude—a Be-Happy Attitude—requires that you let the faith flow free.

"I'm Going to Be a Bridge Builder."

Blessed are the peace-makers, for they shall be called children of God.

HOW WOULD you like to be remembered?

What kind of reputation do you covet? What kind of image do you desire? What words would you wish to be carved on your tombstone?

Do you care? Many would say, "I don't care what people say."

Others might say, "I think it is dangerous to ask questions like these. I might become too self-centered in the process."

But consider: These questions can be very positive and motivational if our objective is to become a truly beautiful human being. For I believe that one thing Jesus is saying in the seventh Beatitude is that happiness comes when we care about our reputation for the right reasons—when we strive to live so that we might be known as "children of God."

"Blessed are the peacemakers, for they shall be *called* the children of God." Now here's a sacred sentence that holds out a hope—and a "how to."

THE HOPE

The hope in this seventh Beatitude is that we might achieve a reputation which will feed our need for self-respect, self-esteem, and self-worth. What is the essence of self-esteem? It's knowing that I have done my best and I am recognized and honored as a child of God!

What do people think of me? How we handle this human question is extremely important. So many of us think of it in terms of being "popular":

- Young people handle this question when they strive to be popular by "going along with the crowd."

- Adults attempt to be popular through their accumulation of material prizes—"keeping up with the Joneses," joining the right clubs, dressing in clothes they believe will win social applause—and through many more social manifestations too many and complex to name.

But I am not really thinking about popularity here—or at least, not *that* kind of popularity. Unless you can maintain an honorable reputation you will not have the kind of popularity that will leave you with a wholesome and healthy sense of self-esteem! The young person who resists the temptation to do drugs feels victorious. He has been a winner! He has been the strongest! He feels good about himself. And such a person will eventually build a positive reputation.

The goal is not just to be popular—but to be popularly recognized as a beautiful human being—a child of God!

- Our attitude shouldn't be: "I don't care what people say."

- Our attitude shouldn't be: "I want to be popular at any price."

- Our attitude—our Be-Happy Attitude—should be: "I will strive so to live that I shall build a reputation as a beautiful child of God!"

THE "HOW TO"

How do we build a reputation as beautiful children of God?

The seventh Beatitude tells us one way: "Blessed are the peacemakers, for they shall be called children of God."

On the morning of my ordination as a minister, I opened

my Bible for my devotions. It fell open to this passage: "You shall be called the repairer of the breach, the restorer of paths to dwell in" (Isa. 58:12, KJV). And I adopted this Bible verse as a direction from my Lord to try to promote a peaceful resolution to any conflict I see. Peacemaking has been one of the important goals of my ministry.

I believe that all of us are called to try to be peacemakers. And being a peacemaker can be extremely rewarding. Helping bring peace where there is tension and conflict and strife brings about a healthy sense of satisfaction, self-esteem, self-worth.

Yet being a peacemaker can be dangerous, too. Playing the role of mediator can be quite costly. We have in my church a few police officers. They've often told me that the most difficult call is a domestic quarrel—one in which a husband and wife are fighting. In such a situation, it's not unusual for the mediator to get shot!

Peacemaking can be a tough role to play. And yet it is absolutely crucial. Ambassador Max Kampelman, who has been instrumental in recent arms negotiations, once quoted Senator Hubert Humphrey on the subject: "Negotiating between conflicting parties is like crossing a river by walking on slippery rocks.... It's risky, but it's the only way to get across."

Being a peacemaker is dangerous. It *is* slippery. You can fall and break your neck. You can drown. But it's the only way to get to the other side. Playing the role of mediator is risky, but it's necessary if breaches are to be repaired.

BREACHES?

We see breaches all around us. In families. Between labor and management. Between nations. Between political parties.

People have said to me, "Schuller, why do you never take stands on controversial political issues?"

I certainly do not feel it is wrong to take a political stand! But I have always felt my special call in political situations is to try to be a repairer of breaches and a restorer of paths. I try to help people get together and resolve their conflicts.

Of course, there are many different ways to solve conflict. I like the story of Helga and Henry, a Swedish couple. They were married for sixty years, and they fought like cats and dogs every day of their married lives. Finally, their sixtieth anniversary arrived. Helga and Henry began the morning with a terrible spat. They argued all day long.

At the end of the day, Helga said to her husband, "Henry, tonight I tink ven ve pray, ve better pray for peace. Ve been fighting each other for sixty years, Henry. May the Lord give us peace. So tonight, I tink I'll pray that the Lord vill take you home and I'll go live with my sister, Olga."

Obviously, that's not the way I would recommend handling a situation of conflict. Most conflicts will be resolved one way or the other. But let us hope and pray that they can be resolved positively and constructively.

When God sees a breach, He builds a bridge. And He calls us to help in the process by being peacemakers.

My friend Hubert Humphrey was a peacemaker. He was a repairer of the breach. He continually inspired me, even in the last few weeks of his life, when he was so very ill.

That is why I hurried to Senator Humphrey's side when his family called me and asked me to come to Minneapolis and encourage him to go back to Washington for a last hurrah.

We conversed a little, then the Lord gave me an idea. I said, "Hubert, when you were really down and depressed in life, how did you get back up?"

I was hoping that in the process of recalling victorious experiences, he would regenerate and recapture the emotion from the reservoirs of his memories, and that this would help him bounce back.

He began recalling several experiences. After a while, I said, "It must have been really difficult for you when you were narrowly defeated by Richard Nixon for the presidency."

He said, "That was probably my toughest time."

"How did you recover emotionally from that?"

I could see the memory reinforcing him and renewing him. Then, when the spark flashed in his eye, I said, "Hubert, when are you going back to Washington again?"

I had caught him off guard, and before he had time to think it through, he said, "Yes, maybe I ought to go back once more."

Muriel Humphrey smiled and said, "That's wonderful. I'll call the President."

Well, I had prayer with him, he walked me to the car, and I went back to the airport and returned home. The next morning I heard on the news that Air Force One, with President Carter, had stopped in Minneapolis, Minnesota, to pick up Hubert Humphrey and take him back to Washington.

He called me later to thank me.

I said, "Hubert, I don't suppose there is any American today who is being applauded more than you."

He said, "That may be true."

"The irony of it is that twenty miles from me sits a man in almost total exile. His name is Richard Nixon. You now are honored. But because of the Watergate scandal, he is suffering the opposite fate. What's your opinion? Should he stay that way all his life? Should he be forgiven? Could there be a healing?"

We discussed it and I said, "I don't think Nixon can make it back without a lot of help: (1) He would have to be invited to a prestigious public event. (2) He would have to be invited to come out by someone all of America respects. (3) He would have to be invited by somebody who is not running for political office, because the opponent would really use this against him."

Senator Humphrey hesitated. Then he said, "It sounds like I'm the man. I'm surely not running for office."

He thought a while and then he said, "Yes, I'll let it be known that he can come to my funeral. I think that will be an event. And since it's being sponsored by a liberal democrat, I don't think they could fault it."

Well, that's exactly what happened. When Senator Humphrey's body lay in its casket under the Capitol rotunda, there sat Muriel Humphrey. And next to Muriel sat Richard Nixon.

Someone said, "How could they invite Nixon to Humphrey's funeral?" Another person sitting near us answered, "If you knew Hubert Humphrey, you wouldn't have asked that question."

"You shall be called a repairer of the breach. And a restorer of paths to dwell in."

BUILD BRIDGES

When God sees a breach, He builds a bridge.

For years this has been my driving spirit. And the spirit behind the drive is what has often been called possibility thinking. In my recent book, *The Power of Being Debt Free,** in chapter four, I put it this way: "Never reject an idea because it will create conflict. Never reject an idea because you have to change your mind or way of doing things. Never

*Coauthored with Paul David Dunn (Nashville: Thomas Nelson Publishers, 1985).

When God
sees a breach . . .
He builds
a bridge!

When He sees
a scar . . .
He creates
a star!

reject an idea because it's going to create problems or it's dangerous or risky."

Possibility thinking says, "Yes!" to an idea if it's going to help people who are in pain. It says "Yes!" to an idea if it holds the prospect of contributing to peace, prosperity, and pride in the human family.

Let me paraphrase again from *The Power of Being Debt Free:* In a world marred by war, poverty, and humiliation in the human family, let there be no offhanded, impulsive rejection of sincere proposals that, however implausible and unrealistic they may seem, do hold some promise of moving the human family closer to prosperity which can eliminate poverty, peace which can eliminate war, and pride which can eliminate human shame.

I really feel we are called by God to be repairers of the breach, restorers of paths to dwell in. Where a relationship has been ripped, torn apart, we are called to bring about reconciliation—where there's a rupture create a rapture. Where there is a scar, create a star; healing where there was only hurt.

WHERE DO WE GET THE POWER FOR PEACE?

The only place you can get that kind of driving spirit, that kind of attitude, is from the Lord. That's why I don't see how proposals for peace can ever happen without divine intervention. For God can provide when all others fail. The power for peace will come when we are reunited with God.

I have in my hand a beautiful book—and a very rare book. It is called *Eighty: An American Souvenir,* and it is by an artist named Eric Sloane, of whom *Reader's Digest* once said, "No man greens the memories of our yesterday with a more bittersweet brush."

I met Eric Sloane one week when I was in New York City, making television appearances. I had an hour between appointments, and I said to my driver, "How far is it to the Armand Hammer Galleries?"

"Oh," he said, "not far." So we stopped in the galleries. In one area was a one-man show by Eric Sloane. The walls were covered with beautiful paintings of sky and covered American bridges.

One customer was looking at a beautiful painting. He looked at me, and whispered to his wife. I knew what they were saying, so I walked over and said hello.

They said, "Oh, Dr. Schuller. We watch you every week." Then they turned to the paintings on the wall. "Isn't his work gorgeous?"

"Yes!"

They said, "It's too bad you weren't here last night, at the opening, because Eric Sloane himself was here."

Just then the door opened. How providential could it be? The couple I had been talking to said, "Oh, here he comes."

I watched a man walk in—ramrod straight, silver-haired.

I spotted dimples and twinkles in the eye, a beautiful blue bow tie, a white shirt, and a double-breasted wool overcoat.

He greeted the customer, who led him over to me. As Mr. Sloane came close, he said, "Dr. Schuller, you look just like you do on television."

He was a friend. He said, "I'll tell you why I've loved your ministry, Dr. Schuller." Then he told me this story:

"I was a very young man when I inherited a million dollars in cash from my father. You wouldn't believe how quickly I spent it all! I woke up one Sunday morning and realized I did not have one dollar left. I was terribly depressed. My inheritance was gone, my father was dead, and I had nothing. I went into a little church—although I was not really very religious—and I heard the minister say, 'God's providence is your inheritance.'

"He didn't know about me.

"But the minister continued, 'God will provide, no matter how bankrupt you are. But you have to trust Him and turn your whole life over to Him.'

"At that time I was just a sign painter. But I took my brush, and underneath my easel I wrote the words, *God's providence is my inheritance*. Once I put that on my easel, my whole life changed."

He continued, "I couldn't be more successful than I am today."

I said, "Would you like to be my guest on *The Hour of Power* some Sunday?"

He enthusiastically replied, "I'd love to be."

Before I left, Sloane held up a book. He said, "Dr. Schuller, this is my autobiography. Most of the copies are still on the boat coming from Italy—that's the only place I trusted to have the printing done."

He added, "I have only six with me, but I want you to have one." And so Eric Sloane autographed one of his books for me for the Schuller library—with a bridge and the date.

That was on Monday. Imagine my shock when I heard three days later that Eric Sloane had died in the streets of New York! So I probably have one of the only autographed copies of his autobiography.

Eric Sloane. In this autobiography he reprinted an etching of a tombstone that could have been his choice for his own tombstone. On it were inscribed these words: "God knows I tried."

What do you want on your tombstone? How do you want to be remembered?

"God's providence is my inheritance." Sloane claimed it. And the same inheritance is waiting for you and me. All we have to do is claim it.

PEACEMAKERS—WHO ARE THEY?

Do you feel bankrupt? Is our country—is our world—bankrupt for power? For peace? God's providence is our inheritance.

How do you want to be remembered? As a child of God? As a peacemaker?

Peacemakers. Who are they? Are they only politicians and world leaders? Or are they also people like you and me?

Everyone can be a peacemaker. The mother who resolves the toy tug-of-war between her toddlers is a peacemaker. The student who helps settle disputes in her dormitory is a peacemaker. The umpire who remains calm in the midst of verbal onslaughts from distraught managers is a peacemaker.

Every one of us can be a peacemaker—no matter who we are and what we do.

I shall never forget when S. Truett Cathy was my guest on *The Hour of Power*. Mr. Cathy is the founder and president of a very successful chain of fast-food restaurants called Chick-Fil-A. On the program, he shared the story of how he had launched this successful business:

"In the early stages of Chick-Fil-A, we were anxious to advertise our product. One day an idea dawned on me. There were competing newspapers in town, and the editors of these papers wouldn't walk on the same side of the street with each other! Since everyone knew about their feud, I invited the two editors to meet with me. I asked each one individually if he'd come down to discuss a full-page ad. Neither one knew I had called the other. When they got there and found themselves face to face with each other, they knew something was up.

"I said, 'If you'll do one thing for me, I'll give both of you a full-page ad. All I want you to do is sit over there in that booth and eat a chicken sandwich together. When you get through, shake hands. Then we'll add the caption, "We disagree on many things, but there's one thing we both agree on: This is the best chicken sandwich we've ever eaten!""'

"Blessed are the peacemakers." In S. Truett Cathy's humorous anecdote, of course, the two editors were just peace *talkers!* What we want to learn to be today is true peace *makers;* like the group of young people I met in Squaw Valley, California.

At that beautiful, snow-covered mountain resort I met the greatest collection of peacemakers I've ever met anywhere—including high-level meetings in Washington, D.C., and around the world. This was not a summit meeting on world peace made up of international delegates. These were young people—hundreds of them—who had gathered to compete in the twelfth annual National Handicapped Ski Championships. They had chosen Squaw Valley for the site of their competition because it had been the 1960 home of the International Winter Olympics.

I had carefully planned my week to include a trip to the Handicapped Nationals because my daughter Carol was skiing in them. As I mentioned in an earlier chapter, Carol lost a leg in a motorcycle accident some years ago. Soon afterward, she became acquainted with the handicapped ski program and decided to become involved. She trained hard for the twelve regional contests in America—all contestants must qualify in the Regionals before they can compete in the Nationals.

I was especially excited about attending the competition because I had never seen Carol ski before. She was scheduled to ski her first race on Thursday, and I was slated to speak in Louisville at the Southern Baptist Convention on Wednesday, so I made plans to fly from Louisville to Squaw Valley in time for the first race on Thursday. However, when the weatherman announced a blizzard was on its way, they moved up the first race to Wednesday, and I missed it. I was terribly disappointed, especially because Carol won the Gold Medal first prize—for the Junior Division in the Downhill. I was very proud of her.

On Friday, the second races were to begin, and my wife and I were there for those. I had never seen so many one-legged people in one place in my life! There were even triple amputees, with two legs and one arm missing. And there were also races for the blind—even a sightless giant slalom. The course all the competitors follow is as long as the one that Olympians ski. No favoritism is shown because competitors are handicapped. There are forty seven gates through which they have to maneuver coming down that mile-long, steep hill.

On Friday the blind were the first to ski. I'd never seen such a race before. The competitors are followed or led down the hill by a sighted person, who shouts directions such as, "Turn to the right. Now to the left. Straight ahead. Quick,

quick, to the right!" This is the way they ski and race. It's an amazing sight.

Then there were the three-trackers. Carol is a three-tracker. The three-trackers ski without a prosthesis, with a ski on their one good leg. They are aided by outriggers—poles with miniature skis on them.

There are also skiers who are below-the-knee amputees, who have complete function of their knee and ski with their prosthesis like normal two-legged skiers. One of those skiers was racing through the course. Carol later related to us, "A funny thing happened yesterday. When the one-legged men skiers were coming down, one of the guys fell and his leg became detached—not from the ski but from his knee. That leg and ski came all the way down the hill and crossed the finish line! The judges didn't know whether they should award the leg or the body up on the hill!" These people have a fantastic sense of humor! They are great peacemakers.

MAKE PEACE — WITH YOURSELF

Why do I call the young people I met at Squaw Valley peacemakers?

When I was a little boy, Adolph Hitler was starting to move through Europe, and people were beginning to talk about the possibility of war. I remember asking my simple, uneducated father, "Dad, what causes wars?"

I never forgot his answer. He said, "Well, somebody gets

mad at somebody. It could be themselves—or even God. They take it out on others. Soon there's a fight. Their friends join in, and before you know it everybody's fighting."

There's a lot of wisdom to that. Years later, when I had the opportunity to study psychology and other advanced disciplines my father never had the benefit of, I saw how right he was. Most wars *do* start because somebody is mad at somebody, and often this angry person is someone who has not accepted himself or his condition. When you can't live with yourself, you will project your inner tension onto others!

The athletes I met at Squaw Valley are peacemakers because they have made peace with themselves and with God. I'm talking about people who have lost legs, arms, sight, mobility. They have every right to be bitter and angry at the world, but they aren't. They look in the mirror, they see what they are, and they accept it. They don't accuse God or anybody else. They are not fixing the blame; they are fixing the problem.

I can't think of many people who have been more of an inspiration to me, in fixing their problem and fixing their world, than Jeff Keith. You may have seen this young man, who lost a leg to cancer. The media covered his phenomenal accomplishment when he finished his historical run across the United States for the American Cancer Society. It took him about two hundred forty days, thirty-six pairs of shoes, and three prosthetic legs, but he made it!

I was with Jeff when his cross-country run was launched at Fennell Hall in Boston, Massachusetts. Both of us spoke at a kick-off prayer breakfast. Teddy Kennedy, Jr., also an amputee, was another speaker. I was very impressed with Jeff's message. He said, "Some people want to move mountains. I've already done that. Now all I want to do is move a country—inspire people to believe they can overcome their problems, too!" That's being a real peacemaker, for in the process of inspiring others to overcome their problems he settles the war going on in the hidden depths of a wounded soul!

Along his three-thousand-mile route, Jeff stopped at several hospitals to visit with depressed and discouraged cancer victims. Time and again young men and women, unable to see beyond their loss, were inspired by Jeff. Several got out of their beds for the first time since their surgery.

But cancer victims weren't the only ones who were helped by Jeff. He also stopped and visited prisoners at Sing Sing. Cell by cell, he talked to them all—this handsome young man with the artificial leg. And the hard-core, maximum-security prisoners were so impressed with him that they held a fund-raising dinner within the prison, with all proceeds going to the American Cancer Society.

I could go on and on about Jeff. He is changing his world for the better. He is fixing the problem. He is a true peacemaker.

LOVE REPAIRS THE BREACH

Peacemakers. They are at peace with themselves, and therefore they can live at peace with others. But as I said before, peacemaking is not always easy. There are times when our own inner conflicts and insecurities hold us back from being "repairers of the breach and restorers of the path."

What helps us then? The restoring power of love.

Burl Ives, the legendary singer, is a happy man—a peacemaker. His secret? He has a big heart full of love. In fact, he's on the President's Committee for the handicapped. Yet, at one time, he found handicapped people challenging and difficult to relate to. Then, about four years ago, something very interesting happened to him that changed his attitude completely. One night at dinner in his Santa Barbara home, Burl explained it to me this way:

"Even though I had worked for many, many years in Washington with the handicapped, if I would see a cerebral palsy victim or maybe a blind person coming down the street—as much as I hate to admit it—I would avoid him or her. Face-to-face encounters with the handicapped frightened me. It was all right to sing and entertain, but when it came down to one-to-one, I managed to slip off to the side.

"But one day, when I was in Santa Barbara walking down to the docks, I noticed a group of children with a teacher some distance away. I paid no attention. I was walking along when all at once one of the little boys broke away from the teacher and ran to me. He clasped me around the knees and

"God
Loves You
And So
Do I"

. . . *a prescription*

for peacemaking

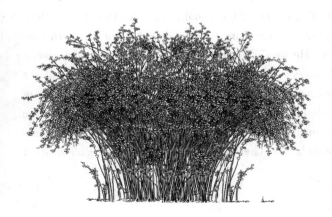

began to embrace me. There was this little boy, who obviously suffered from muscular spasms, and here we were face to face. I knelt down and I saw through to the boy. I saw his eyes and his soul, and there I encountered love—love for me. It had a great effect on me. Since then, I don't pass on the other side of the road."

What was it that kept Burl Ives from making peace with the handicapped? He was afraid of them. And as Gerald Jampolsky has said, "The opposite of love is not hate. The opposite of love is fear." So the opposite of peace is deeper than just conflict—the opposite of peace is insecurity.

Burl Ives was afraid that he wouldn't be able to handle these handicapped kids or his feelings about them, and so he was held back from being a peacemaker. Yet he discovered, through the love of a child, that there was nothing to fear.

If we are to create peace in this world, we must understand what the issue really is. It's not love versus hate, or war versus peace. It's love versus fear and insecurity!

Willard Scott, the humorist and weatherman for the NBC *Today* show, the original Ronald McDonald and Bozo the clown, is a walking, talking definition of the word *happiness*. He says, "When I was a clown, I found that everybody loves a clown, no matter who the clown is. If you're a Democrat or a Republican, if you're Catholic, Protestant, or Jewish, it doesn't matter if you're a clown. It dawned on me that one of the things about being a clown is that you have no labels. There are no preconceived ideas about what this clown is, what he thinks about, or what he's related to.

"I have found that I can have a lay ministry on television just by trying to convey positive thoughts—love, really. I was raised in a Southern Baptist church and I remember our old preacher, Dr. Campbell. The thing I loved about him most was that he radiated love. His sermons were good, sometimes. Sometimes they were not the greatest. But you could always count on him whenever you needed someone to care for you. When someone died or someone got sick, Dr. Campbell was always there.

"And I remember when I was a little child of four or five years, after church all the kids would come out of the church. Dr. Campbell was six-foot-five—a big man—and wore a cutaway Prince Albert. He would sweep us little kids up in his arms and hug and love us. I believe that that kind of personal love and personal care and consideration had a tremendous influence on my life—as, of course, did my own mother and father, who adored and loved me and gave me everything that I could ever ask for. I do believe that no matter what our problems are, we can all love each other. We can share each other's lives. We can make our world better by being positive, and that's what I try to do."

A SONG OF PEACE

You may say, "That doesn't work on the international level." But let me tell you a true story—the story of Roland Hayes.

Some of you young people may not realize that his was undoubtedly one of the great voices of the twentieth century; he was a tremendous concert soloist. And he had all the odds against him. He said once, "My mother is the person who taught me how to think positively, and I owe all of my success to her."

Roland Hayes was one of three children born to a black family on a fifteen-acre cotton farm in Tennessee. When Roland was five years old, his father was caught under a branch while felling a tree and was killed. The mother tried as best she could to train and raise her three boys on their small plot of land. One day she called the boys together and said, "Boys, you just have to get an education. I have a plan. We are going to hitch up the wagon, go to Chattanooga, get a job, and see to it that you boys get an education."

The next day they hitched up their one horse to the wagon and Roland's mother rode in it. The three boys walked barefoot the sixty-two miles to Chattanooga, Tennessee.

While the family was living in Chattanooga, they sang in a church choir there. And one day the choir director, Mr. Calhoun, played for them a recording of Caruso and of Melba, two of the great singers of the day. Roland Hayes was so moved by the music that he said, "I believe that God has called me to sing a message of peace and brotherhood around the world." With that inspiration he went on to get a job and then enrolled at Fisk University.

While traveling with the college concert singers a few

years later in Boston, Roland had a sudden impulse which, to his dying day, he said was from God—to drop out and try to get established in Boston. Constantly recurring in his memory were the words of his mother, "Roland, you can do it if you believe you can and if you give your life to God." He got a job as a hotel porter, earned seven dollars a week, brought his mother up to Boston, and rented a little apartment which cost him almost his whole week's pay. He used orange crates for furniture.

Roland reasoned that he would never get anyplace unless he made a name for himself, so he decided to give a concert—all on his own—in the biggest and the best place, the main auditorium in Boston.

As he said years later, "I found out nobody ever did anything for me unless I really stuck my neck out and tried to help myself." He tried to find people to sponsor him, but no one would do it because he was a nobody. He thought and thought and he prayed.

Suddenly the bright idea came. He wrote a letter to all the richest people in Boston introducing himself as Roland Hayes, one of the great concert artists of the future, and inviting them to his first public American concert on such and such a date—tickets, $1.50.

The impossible happened: Roland Hayes single-handedly sold out every seat in the auditorium. The concert was a great success. He personally made two thousand dollars cash. In addition, someone in the audience from Santa Monica,

California, invited him to the West Coast to give a concert. He gratefully accepted.

After the Santa Monica performance a music critic approached the young singer and said, "Mr. Hayes, when you sang, you stirred me, as do all of the great concert artists. But you had something more, and I cannot put my finger on it."

That night in his hotel room Roland was haunted by the man's comment. What did he have that others didn't have? Could it be his blood? He remembered his old uncle saying to him as they picked cotton, "Roland, your father and me came from Africa, from a line of chiefs. Don't you ever forget that. You got chief's blood in your veins." (It takes a strong self-image—positive self-esteem—to dare to be a peacemaker.)

As Roland Hayes prayed that night in Santa Monica, he had a revelation that he would leave the United States and go to East Africa to try to find the tribe from which he came and discover what made him unique. He spent the last of his money from the Boston concert to get to London, England, on his way to Africa. In England, however, his money ran out.

A friend of the pastor of the Royal Chapel inquired, "Roland, how would you like to sing for my pastor friend on Sunday?"

Roland accepted quickly. In the Royal Chapel that Sunday he sang the spiritual, "And He Never Spoke a Mumbling Word."

Three days later Roland got a telephone call from a friend, who asked, "Have you heard the news?"

"No. What?"

"Well, you sang in the Royal Chapel Sunday, and do you know who was there?" Roland remained silent. "The King and the Queen of England! And they are requesting a command performance at Buckingham Palace."

Roland couldn't believe his ears. Two days later he sang for the King and Queen, and in the audience were both Caruso and Melba, whose recordings had first inspired him to pursue a singing career.

Roland Hayes became an overnight success. That year—1924—looked wonderful for him. He was even booked for a concert at the Beethoven Concert Hall in Berlin. This concert would undoubtedly establish him as a concert soloist on the continent of Europe. En route to Germany, Roland stopped in Prague. He was called into the American consul's office. "Mr. Hayes," the consul said, "I have bad news for you. You are going to have to cancel your concert in Germany. The French have taken over the Rhineland and they are holding it with troops made up of Negroes brought from America. The Germans are furious. No black-skinned person will be able to sing in Germany at this time."

"Thank you for telling me this, Mr. Consul," Roland said. "I will surely pray about it." The days passed and he could not bring himself to cancel the concert.

On the night of the concert, Roland and his black

accompanist carefully made their way to the auditorium and slipped in through a back door. Once inside, they peered through the curtains and saw that the place was packed to overflowing. Now Roland realized he was an internationally controversial case.

When the curtain went up, Roland Hayes stood in the curve of the baby grand piano, his accompanist seated at the piano beside him. He quietly folded his hands, looked upward, and spoke a private prayer to God: "God, make me a horn for the Omnipotent to sound through."

As he stood silently praying, suddenly he heard hissing, then stomping, and then the catcalls and boos. Somebody shouted, "Don't disgrace the Beethoven Concert Hall with plantation songs about black men from America." Hate seemed to fill that auditorium. His accompanist said, "Mr. Hayes, we better get out of here."

Objects began to fly onto the stage, narrowly missing the soloist. Roland Hayes later recalled the incident and remarked, "I just stood there with my hands folded and prayed, 'God, what will I do?'"

A bright idea entered his mind. To the accompanist he said, without taking his eyes off the audience, "Let's begin with Beethoven's 'This Is My Peace.'" The accompanist picked out the music for this God-inspired first number, and slowly, softly the fingers began to roll across the piano. A surprised murmur ran through the hall as the German concert-goers heard the music of their favorite, Beethoven.

Roland Hayes opened his mouth and began to sing "This Is My Peace." His mighty voice rolled through the auditorium, and the audience quieted down. By the time he finished, there was absolute attention. He went on to sing several classical numbers and ended the concert with Negro spirituals, the plantation songs. At the close of the concert, some members of the audience jumped up on the stage, hoisted Roland on their shoulders, and paraded him around the auditorium. He was the hero of the continent, and he was an inspiration in settling the dispute between France and Germany.

THE PRINCE OF PEACE

"Blessed are the peacemakers, for they shall be called children of God."

Who are the peacemakers? They are not necessarily the people who are *talking* about peace all the time. Peacemakers are those who are *doing* something, creating something, building something—bridges, mostly!

Maybe peacemakers are people like you and me who, in our own ways, are trying to bring Jesus Christ into human hearts.

Do you want peace in your family? Do you want peace in your community? Do you want peace with other races and other cultures? There will not be peace anywhere as long as there is a war going on in your heart and in your soul.

So how do you make peace with yourself? You make

peace with yourself by meeting the greatest peacemaker of all time, Jesus Christ. He was called "the Prince of Peace." He lived, He died on a Friday we call Good Friday, and He rose again on Easter. He's alive today. He is my closest personal friend.

"Blessed are the peacemakers, for they shall be called children of God." You can be a peacemaker once you have your life together, once you've let Jesus become your friend. When Jesus is your friend, you have an internalized positive self-image. You become a possibility thinker and you begin to say, "I can do all things because I am somebody. I am a friend of Jesus Christ."

That's a great way to live. And that's why most Christians are relaxed persons. They're not uptight. And they don't carry around a bundle of emotional garbage that shows itself in the form of anxiety, fear, tension, or insecurity. They are not angry people who feel they're victims of the world's injustices.

I made a trip to Mainland China a few years ago, and my son led a tour of people who were invited to be a part of that mission. One night in Shanghai, I tapped on my son's door. It was rather late, but Bob was not in his room. Someone said, "He went out for a walk."

I immediately went out into the street to see if I could spot him. I saw a crowd—almost a mob—gathered on a nearby bridge. I cautiously approached the large group of Chinese and saw, in the midst of them, a six-foot-four-inch

American. It was my son. Bob was talking to two of the leaders of this great crowd. I could see that he was excitedly sharing Christ with these two.

Afraid of intruding, I quietly retreated to the hotel. Later that night he told me what happened. He had been standing on the bridge (more important, he was about to build a bridge), and two bright young students had come up to him. They were university students who spoke English.

"Who are you?" the students asked my son. "Where are you from? What are you doing here?"

Bob said, "I'm a Christian. Have you ever heard about Jesus Christ?"

They said, "What's a Christian? Who is Jesus Christ?"

He told them, and he led them through some basic spiritual truths. He explained that Christianity teaches that God wants us all to be beautiful persons. It's a law of life that we all have our sins, our internal tensions. We all need salvation. And then he said "Jesus came to save us."

He asked them if they'd like to accept Jesus as their friend. To his amazement, they said, "Yes."

So Bob prayed with them. There on the bridge in Shanghai, Bob and the young Chinese students prayed together. Bob told them about the Bible and, in response to their request, he later sent them Bibles and continued corresponding with them. What Bob was doing was a special kind of peacemaking.

Yes, all of us can be peacemakers—wherever we are.

There may be a tension inside of you, in your home, or in your place of business. But you can resolve this tension if you give it all you've got. Tackling the problem of tension is no different than tackling any other problem. You can make peace in much the same way that you solve other problems. The people who ultimately win at what they go after are the people who give it all they've got.

Let me share with you one of the most inspiring sights that I've ever seen. It happened on the slopes of Squaw Valley. The handicapped skier's name was Kim Caulfield. She was about eighteen and blind. Kim was being led down the giant slalom. She made it through forty-four gates, and she was lined up straight with the finish line. Her guide behind her said, "Straight ahead Kim; go for it!"

Kim dug in and was flying over the snow when she hit a rut. The poles flew out of her hands. She fell flat on her stomach. She knew she'd have to get her body across the finish line or be disqualified. She looked beaten, but she didn't stop. She reached out for her poles. When she couldn't find them, she started swimming over the snow, straight ahead, until she crossed the finish line.

"Kim, you made it!" the judge called out. But she didn't hear him. She just kept swimming over the snow flat on her stomach for another five—ten—fifteen feet.

The judge kept shouting, "You made it, Kim; you can stop!" She still didn't hear. Finally a second voice, then another, then all of us who were spectators shouted, "You made it, Kim!"

Kim stopped, still flat on her belly. Then she heard the applause. She jumped up to her feet and danced for joy.

You can do it, too! You can be a peacemaker if you choose to believe in yourself and in Christ.

"I CAN CHOOSE TO BE HAPPY—ANYWAY!"

Blessed are those who are persecuted for righteousness' sake, for theirs is the kingdom of heaven.

THE LAST BE-HAPPY Attitude. The final lesson.

Jesus saves His toughest teaching for last. Only those who have gone through all the previous classes are qualified for admittance to this final lesson: "Blessed are those who are persecuted for righteousness' sake."

HOW TO BE HAPPY

Be-Happy Attitude #1 was: "*I need help—I can't do it alone!*" In order to be truly happy, I must learn to admit those areas in which I am weak and to welcome constructive help and advice.

Be-Happy Attitude #2: *"I'm really hurting—but I'm going to bounce back!"* In the face of failure or loss, I must have the attitude that I'm going to grow from my experience and move on.

Be-Happy Attitude #3: *"I'm going to remain cool, calm, and corrected."* I must maintain a steady, stable, teachable attitude through the good times and the bad times before I will ultimately find true satisfaction.

Be-Happy Attitude #4: *"I really want to do the right thing!"* My attitude must be to achieve, maintain, and live by integrity, for honesty and righteousness attract good friends and great people who will help me. Here is the sensible secret of sane and safe ego control.

Be-Happy Attitude #5: *"I'm going to treat others the way I want others to treat me."* I will have a positive attitude, keeping in mind that there is a law of proportionate return. So when I am abused or mistreated, I shall choose to be merciful and forgiving, knowing that this will come back to me in kind and I will be blessed.

Be-Happy Attitude #6: *"I've got to let the faith flow free through me."* I must constantly scrutinize my motives, my methods, and my manners, being humble enough to know that I can get on the wrong track in a hurry. So, I shall maintain a positive, soul-searching attitude toward myself at all times, lest I get off the track and miss getting on the best track of all.

Be-Happy Attitude #7: *"I'm going to be a bridge builder."*

To be truly happy, I shall maintain the attitude that an enemy can become a valuable friend. I shall strive as much as I can to live in respect and harmony and peace with all people. But this will mean making peace with myself first!

This brings us to the last Be-Happy Attitude— #8: *"I can choose to be happy anyway!"* If, after applying all of these positive attitudes to the best of my ability, I still find myself the abused victim in human relationships—personal, social, or professional—I shall choose to believe that God can settle the score in His way and in His time. I shall be blessed by knowing that my hurts, borne quietly, patiently, and positively, can be turned into halos.

STICKS AND STONES CAN BREAK YOUR BONES— BUT WORDS HURT, TOO!

Persecution is something all of us have faced or will face. For some—especially in certain countries—persecution takes the form of physical torture. Through the years it has been everything from the rack to bamboo under the fingernails to cigarette burns and electric shock. With terrorism on the march today, this subject becomes painfully relevant.

And persecution wears many faces! It is true that we in the free countries are not constantly shadowed by the threat of physical persecution for our beliefs. But at one time or another we can all expect to face some kind of harassment, snubs, rejection, or discrimination. Emotional persecution that attacks a person's self-esteem can be devastating! The calculated insult, the contrived put-down are weapons wielded even by religious people against their own kind.

Yes, persecution occurs at various levels in life and strikes from a variety of sources. Our supporters can inexplicably turn on us. (Judas was Christ's treasurer.)

Society can snub and turn its back on us.

When we fail to live up to our expectations, we often persecute ourselves. Regrets, guilt, remorse can torture the soul! Is any form of persecution more prevalent and widespread than self-recrimination?

Persecution attacks losers and winners, too! Even the achiever has enemies, people who are jealous and would "persecute." Excellence takes it on the chin today. Positive thinkers have always been persecuted. They said of Norman Vincent Peale, "Peale is appalling, but Paul is appealing." Clever, cute, but very Un-Christian! Negative thinkers persecute positive thinkers. Rich people are persecuted, too, by suspicious, cynical "have nots" who assume that anyone who is wealthy must be a crook or a swindler. Super-successful people are often viewed with suspicion; persecution at that level is very prevalent in society.

Peer pressure can be a powerful persecution. The truth is: No social unit, no racial or religious community, and no age grouping is free from the sometimes blatant and more-often subtle stabs of persecution. Young people are often led into drugs and immoral conduct under the fear of persecuting taunts from their classmates. Social pressures in junior high, high school, and college are often applied to those who live by high ideals. The square and straight person can expect to be laughed at and scorned. Insulting epithets, chilly ridicule, and demeaning labels become weapons of emotional torture.

Do you feel persecuted? Then be of good cheer! You can choose to be happy—anyway. This Be-Happy Attitude is for you. Yes! You can be happy, too, even if you are the innocent victim of authentic injustice, insult, injury, discrimination, or oppression.

How can you be happy when you are facing persecution? Is this Be-Happy Attitude really practical? Is it possible? Oh, yes. There are several people I know who have gone through tremendous suffering, and they have emerged from the fire not unscathed, but stronger.

Follow with me and you will see how they did it, and how you, too, can turn your scars into stars. These people who have mastered this final Be-Happy Attitude were able to be victorious because they:

(1) *Remained POSITIVE!* They took a positive attitude— they chose to rejoice in spite of their circumstances.

(2) *Were PREPARED!* They had equipped themselves with a spiritual and emotional support system that became an invisible shield.

(3) *PERSEVERED in doing what is right.* They kept on

211

keeping on, and would not let others get the better of them.

(4) *PARDONED those who hurt them!* They forgave those who did the persecuting.

(5) *PERSISTED in trusting God,* even when He seemed far away! They kept in mind that God is the ruler yet, that He will have the last word and it will be good.

(6) *PRAYED for understanding and strength!* They accepted the help God offers to those who are suffering. They understood that they were not the only ones who had ever been persecuted, and so they resisted the temptation to fall victim to the persecution complex and martyr syndrome.

(7) *PASSED triumphantly through the necessary PHASES* that we must all go through when we face tragedy!

STAY POSITIVE

Dr. Viktor Frankl, an eminent psychiatrist and author of the famous book, *Man's Search for Meaning,* is a living example of this Be-Happy Attitude.

Dr. Frankl, who is a Jew, was imprisoned by the Nazis in the Second World War. His wife, his children, and his parents were all killed in the holocaust.

The Gestapo took Viktor and made him strip. He stood there totally naked. But they noticed that he still had on his wedding band. As they removed even that from him, he said to himself, "You can take away my wife, you can take away my children, you can strip me of my clothes and my freedom, but there is one thing no person can *ever* take away from me—and that is my freedom to choose how I will react to what happens to me!"

That was the birth of an idea that years later he would develop into "logotherapy," a form of therapy that has helped countless thousands deal with what life hands them. And that basic lesson in positive reactionism remains the keystone in the whole arch of possibility thinking. My philosophy has been greatly shaped and influenced by Dr. Frankl's lectures, writings, and private meetings with him.

We are free to choose our attitude in any given situation—to maintain a positive attitude no matter how negative the situation. What a life-changing idea! Dr. Smiley Blanton, another great psychiatrist, once told of listening to a patient who was depressed. After several sessions he interrupted this suffering soul: "'*If only*'— that's your problem!" He explained, "You keep repeating those words, '*If only* I had . . .' '*If only* I hadn't . . .' My prescription for you is to strike those words from your life! Replace them with the words, '*next time.*' Do not deny the reality of mistakes made or sins committed, but learn to forgive yourself. You can do that by facing the torturing memories with a positive attitude, affirming, '*next time* things are going to be different.'" Great advice to a victim of self-persecution!

Here then is a Be-Happy Attitude that we can all use:

"Blessed are those who are persecuted for righteousness' sake, for theirs is the kingdom of heaven. Blessed are you when men revile you and persecute you and utter all kinds of evil against you falsely on my account. Rejoice and be glad, for your reward is great in heaven" (Matt. 5:10–11).

Jesus was saying much the same thing Viktor Frankl said: You can choose to take a positive attitude toward your persecution. And if you can do this, you will eventually triumph. This lesson in dealing with persecution is a lesson every Christian must learn, because everyone is going to face a time when he has to stand up for what he believes and run the risk of rejection or ridicule. If we learn this lesson well, we'll be able to tolerate rejection and *our self-esteem will be enhanced in the process.*

That's a Be-Happy Attitude! If we don't have a positive attitude, rejection will devastate our dignity. And it's impossible to be happy without a strong self-respect!

BE PREPARED

We make a grave mistake if we assume that we will never face persecution simply because we live in a free country. There is a strong probability that *all* of us will face some kind of persecution at one time or another in our lives. And it is vitally important to spiritually arm ourselves with inner emergency equipment *before* the crises hit.

Most of us have emergency equipment in our homes and offices—a first-aid kit, a flashlight, perhaps a fire extinguisher, at least a telephone with which to call an emergency unit. We prepare for emergencies before they hit, for we never know when they will come and what they will do to us.

As we need to be prepared with physical equipment, we also need to be prepared spiritually *before* times of persecution arrive. We do that by spending time daily—or, at the very least, weekly—in positive praying, positive Bible study, and worshipping regularly at a positive-thinking church. We saturate our subconscious minds with positive Bible verses, positive hymns, and examples of people who made it through trials successfully, with their faith intact.

Before we can pass the test and graduate from the school of discipleship and commence living out the Christian faith in a secular and sinful society, we have to pass this final exam: We must be spiritually and psychologically conditioned for ridicule, rejection, and persecution. Only those who have learned that they can expect persecution and are prepared to maintain a positive attitude through hard or horrific times will prove to be star ambassadors of Jesus Christ in the world.

So, study the rest of this chapter carefully. It is a first aid kit for unexpected crises. In it you will find positive Bible verses, positive hymns, and stories of people who have triumphed in the face of enormous persecution.

215

PERSEVERE IN DOING
WHAT IS RIGHT

Today, the social and moral pressures in our pluralistic society threaten the Christian as never before! The temptation to "become like" the nonreligious persons around us can be terribly intimidating! The temptation to adopt the value system of a secular society becomes a deadly serious form of insidious persecution. To my Christian reader: A warning! Compromise and abandon your principles, and you will literally lose your soul; you'll no longer be the person you were before. You will have lost your identity as a distinctive, independent person.

For when you give in, for fear of ridicule, to the pressure to be like everyone else, you'll have allowed yourself to be absorbed in the total collective society. Run with the foxes, dash with the hounds, and become just another part of the mass of humanity. You'll be a nothing! A no one! Yes, a non-individual! Only a blob absorbed in a mass! For a little bit of you dies every time you surrender a cherished ideal, abandon a noble value, or discard a moral principle.

So then, how do we stand up against social persecution? Once there was a politician who did the best job he could. But, being human, he made mistakes and was criticized, and reporters repeated errors of fact about him in the paper. Well, he became so upset that he drove out into the country to visit his dear friend, a farmer. "What am I going to do?" the politician cried. "I've tried so hard. Nobody has tried harder than

I have to do more good for more people—and look how they criticize me!"

But the old farmer could hardly hear the complaint of his persecuted politician friend because his hound dog was barking at the full moon. The farmer rebuked his dog, but the dog kept barking. Finally the farmer said to the politician, "Do you want to know how you should handle your unfair critics? Here's how. Listen to that dog. Now, look at that moon. And remember that people will keep yelling at you— they'll nip at your heels, and they'll criticize you. But here's the lesson: *The dog keeps howling, but the moon keeps shining!"*

Let people persecute you—but don't stop doing all the good you've been doing.

Think of the great names: Joan of Arc, Martin Luther King, Stephen, Paul. These names remind us of the final, ultimate Be-Happy Attitude. For these people were really blessed. Even in the face of persecution, they were blessed, because they stood fast for what they believed. They persevered in doing right.

How were these great men and women able to "keep shining" in the face of persecution? They were given the most precious gift of all—the assurance that no matter what happens—even death—nothing can come between us and God's love. "Neither death, nor life, nor angels, nor principalities, nor things present, nor things to come, nor powers, nor height, nor depth, nor anything else in all creation, will

*If you think
you're a total failure,
remember this:*

*Your greatest
successes . . . will
forever remain . . .
God's secret!*

be able to separate us from the love of God in Christ Jesus.... We are *more than conquerors* through him who loved us" (Rom. 8:39, 38).

What does this mean to us? What could top being a conqueror? What is better than winning? Why, it is converting your opponent to your side. It is turning an adversary into an ally. It is turning an enemy into a friend. That is being *more than a conqueror!*

Jesus did this. When He was persecuted by the Roman centurion, He did not lash back at him, nor did He threaten him. Instead, He won him over with forgiving love. Even as Jesus died, the centurion exclaimed, "Truly this was the Son of God" (Matt. 27:54).

There is something nobler than winning. There is something more rewarding than conquering. It is possible to be more than a conqueror. You may not live to see it, but you had better believe that when you maintain a positive attitude in the face of persecution and persevere in doing what is right, you will be blessed.

PARDON THOSE WHO HAVE HURT YOU

"Not easy," you say. And you are right. One of the most difficult things to do is to forgive someone who has hurt you. Again, we take a lesson from Jesus in dealing positively with our persecution.

When he was on the cross, stripped of his dignity, Jesus cried out, "Father, forgive them, for they know not what they do!"

Sometimes it is *humanly* impossible to forgive. When that happens, we need to call upon divine intervention. We ask God to forgive those who hurt us and to work on our hearts so that we can eventually see our hurt from their perspective.

Frequently, more often than not, people who hurt others through their words or their actions are unaware that they've injured anybody. They "know not what they do."

Other times, they are incapable of being held account-able for their actions. "They know not what they do" in terms of being so mixed up, so troubled, so spiteful, or so insecure that they act purely out of gut instinct. They are incapable of thinking about others' feelings or others' lives.

Have you been hurt? Are you still carrying that pain within? Is it impossible to forgive and forget? Then start by saying the prayer Christ prayed: "Father, forgive them, for they know not what they do."

PERSIST IN TRUSTING GOD

When we are suffering, it is tempting to lash out at everyone around us—including God. And it is hard to keep on trusting Him when we are being rejected or ridiculed. But if we are to be victorious in the face of persecution, it is vital to maintain our trust in Him.

The Book of Job has been hailed by students of literature as one of the greatest epic poems ever written. But it is far more than a beautiful piece of literature. Job is a story of triumphal trust—for surely nobody has ever faced more persecution than Job.

"When he has tried me, I shall come forth as gold" (Job 23:10).

"Though he slay me, yet will I trust in him" (Job 13:15, KJV).

Both of these statements made by Job *after* he faced persecution are testimonial to the fact that he successfully endured his persecution. Job illustrates a faith that will not lose its grip, a faith that never lets go.

Let's examine Job's trials. He was very rich. He had three thousand camels, which would be like having a few hundred Rolls-Royces today. He had seven sons and three daughters. His fame was worldwide. He was what you could call super-rich, super-successful. At the age of thirty-nine, he had it made. And on top of everything, he had a reputation for being religious.

One day, according to the book of Job, the devil appeared to the Almighty and said, "So, you think Job's such a good guy? Let me tell you—it is easy to have faith when you're rich like that. The truth is that Job only comes across with a smiling, happy faith because life is easy for him. He's rich. But if he were poor and suffering, then we'd see what kind of faith Job really has."

In this epic poem God agrees that the devil can try Job. The first thing that happens to him is financial ruin. He loses all of his property. The next thing that happens is that his house collapses and all of his children are killed. Then once the money is gone, Job's opportunistic friends go. He's lost his money, his family, and his power; the community just doesn't respond to him anymore. Finally one day he sits in the ashes, naked. And he says, "Naked I came from my mother's womb, and naked shall I return; the Lord gave, and the Lord has taken away; blessed be the name of the Lord" (Job 1:21).

Then he adds this inspiring pledge: "When he has tried me, I shall come forth as gold!" (Job 23:10). It is the same faith that I describe in the Possibility Thinker's Creed: "When faced with a mountain, I will not quit! I will keep on striving until I climb over, find a pass through, tunnel underneath, or simply stay and turn the mountain into a gold mine with God's help."

This is the kind of faith we used to sing about in a hymn:

> *Oh, for a faith that will not shrink,*
> *though pressed by every foe—*
> *That will not stumble on the brink*
> *of any earthly woe;*
> *A faith that shines forth bright and clear*
> *when troubles rage about;*
> *A faith that in the darkest time*
> *will know no doubt.*
> —William Bathurst

Such was the faith that Job had: "Though God slay me, yet will I trust him."

This faith is sensational! Fantastic! Awesome! And it's exciting to study it in depth because it puts us squarely face to face with three questions concerning persecution.

The first is, "How do human beings react to persecution?"

The second question is, "What is the nature of this trust that Job sustained?"

And the final question is, "Is it possible for you to acquire that same positive mental trust?"

Consider the first question: "How do human beings react to persecution?" The answer is threefold: (a) The most common negative reaction is simply to give up and accept defeat. I call people who react like this CINDERS.

(b) The second common reaction is equally negative. Consider the SINNERS. What is a sinner? A sinner is somebody who deliberately chooses to abandon all faith. A sinner is somebody who by an act of choice takes the negative reaction. The ultimate sin—what is it? It's choosing to be a cynic, choosing not to believe.

(c) One reaction is seen in the *cinders*—the *burned-out* people. The second reaction is seen in the sinners—they're the *burned-up* people; they become angry at God and everybody else. Finally, there are the SENDERS. They don't get burned out. They don't get burned up. They just burn brighter—and shine like gold!

223

Three reactions to suffering:

1. *Some are Cinders . . . they get burned–OUT!*

2. *Some are Sinners . . . they get burned–UP!*

3. *Some are Senders…they just burn BRIGHTER!*

That's the way it was with Job when he was tested and tried. He did indeed glow with the golden light of inspiring faith.

The senders. They burn bright and send out a light in the darkness that says, "Watch me, world! I may be tested! Tried! Persecuted! But I still trust God." They send out a message to the world that you can believe in God even when He is silent. The amazing thing is this: The darker the suffering, the brighter the message that the sender shares with everyone.

The principle is best illustrated by a sight I witnessed while flying over the Pacific Ocean. I thought I'd seen the wake of every possible boat or ship. I've seen the gorgeous wakes of luxury cruise liners, and I've seen the lovely little wake of a canoe on a quiet stream in Canada. I've watched my children ski behind a motorboat in glassy wakes on an early morning mountain lake.

Long or short, narrow or wide—it's always been a thrilling sight to me to look back and see the wake that's left behind. But flying over the ocean I saw a wake such as I've never seen before. I saw it from the window of a commercial jet. At first I thought the marks on the water were hidden reefs. But my companion said, "It looks like the wake of a vessel, but those lines are too far apart to be that!"

As we flew on, we could see that the lines were in fact moving closer together, the way a wake would look. And finally we saw the vessel that created the wake. What had

225

made this mammoth wake? Was it an aircraft carrier? No. It was just a very slim, slender, black, short line in the water with a periscope piercing the surface.

I said, "It's a submarine!"

My companion said, "It is, at that."

It had just surfaced. And a submarine, when it surfaces after plowing through the depths, leaves a wake that is remarkable.

I tell you today: People who go through the deep waters of suffering leave a wide wake if they choose (and it is a choice) to trust and forgive. In spite of their suffering, they send a huge message of hope to the world.

What are the reactions you can choose in the face of suffering? You can burn out, burn up, or burn bright! You can be a *cinder,* a *sinner,* or a *sender.* Your reaction must be to trust God—anyway! Your reaction must be to forgive—anyway! When the suffering is horrific, then *trust and forgiveness are your only positive options. All of the other possible choices are negative.* Don't be a cinder. Don't be a sinner. Do be a sender!

The first question I've already asked and answered is:

"How do people react to suffering?" The second question is: "What is this trust, really?" It's really quite simple: Trust is the belief that God is alive anyway!

I've said it before, but it bears repeating. Scrawled in the basement of a German home was a Star of David next to these words:

I believe in the sun even when it is not shining.
I believe in love even when I do not feel it.
I believe in God even when He is silent.

God is alive. Even though you may not be hearing Him or feeling Him do not discard Him.

The truth of this statement came through to me with renewed power in an amusing incident that happened to me several years ago. That week, I lectured on Tuesday at the University of Berkeley, and I was scheduled to speak on Wednesday to the Lutherans in Arizona on the five-hundredth anniversary of Martin Luther's birth. On Thursday I was to be at Northwestern College in Iowa, and on Friday I had to be at Johns Hopkins in Baltimore. As you can see, it was really a tightly scheduled week. Everything was carefully timed and planned. If I missed a connection, I would really be in trouble.

Everything went smoothly until I got to Phoenix to catch my eastbound plane. I was first at the check-in desk, to make sure that I would not be late. Soon there was a line of about thirty or forty people behind me with all their suitcases, waiting to check in. The plane was scheduled to leave in thirty minutes. Eventually the lady came to start the check-in. She looked harassed. Trying to be understanding, I said, "You look as though you have troubles."

She didn't even look up to see my face. She just mumbled, "Boy, have I got troubles!" She said, "I suppose you're here to check in on this flight to Denver."

227

I said, "Yes."

She said, "Well, I just got word that that flight's going to be canceled, and I suppose you are now going to want me to help you, which I'm obligated to do, but I don't know what I'm going to do!" Then she looked up and said, "Oh! Dr. Schuller!" And she took hold of my hands and added, "Say a little prayer for me; I'm in trouble. I don't know what I'm going to do. Let me talk to the computer for a minute."

She began to type on the keyboard, then she stopped and looked at the screen. Her face registered dismay and frustration. Frantic, she picked up the phone, "Ben! Help! The computer's dead! Nothing! It's just looking at me. You say we have a line problem? I don't care if it is a line problem. Make it come alive, *please!*"

The point is this: Some of you complain when God is silent, and doubt His existence. However, you don't stop believing in computers when one is silent because there's a line problem. Don't stop believing in God because you're not hearing from Him at the moment.

What was this trust that Job had? Job trusted that God was still alive, even though He seemed silent in the face of his persecution. But there's a second element to this trust. The second element is that God will have the last word. What you are facing now will not last forever. It is merely a phase in your life. It's not the end of the story.

Oral Roberts went through a horrific tragedy a few years ago when his son was found dead. I sent him a telegram, which said, "Dear Oral, first let me quote you: *God knows a lot more about this than we do*. And now, Oral, may I add my own line, *God will have the last word, and it will be GOOD!"*

Don't blame God, don't lash out in bitterness at Him. Even though He may have allowed your suffering, He never *caused* it. He can help you turn it into something beautiful if you will remember that God is not finished with you—yet. Know that God will have the last word, that this suffering you are going through is not the last word. It is a passage, not a dead end.

What is the best possible reaction to persecution? The answer is: Trust is the only sensible response.

And what is this trust? This trust is that God is alive, even if He's silent. It is the trust that God will come back "on the line" and His last word will be good.

Now we come to the third question: "How can we trust God in times of suffering?"

Let me give you two positive thoughts. The first positive thought is this: Can you trust the banker if he has all his own money in the bank? Of course. And the same is true with God. God has a lot more to lose than you do. Really, it wasn't Job alone who was on trial. God was also on trial.

Every time you face suffering, remember that you are on trial, but so is the Almighty. He must come forth as gold too. His honor is at stake. At worst, all you could lose is your life or soul. But God could lose His honor. After all, He has made Promises. His Word is filled with them.

Possibility thinking can turn persecution into opportunities: for healing, for forgiveness, for compassion!

There is a second positive thought to keep in mind in the tough times that test our faith. What kept Job's trust going? He was an upright, honorable man. If your heart is right, your faith will burn bright. You can trust Him if you know you've done—and are doing—the best you could—or can.

PRAY FOR UNDERSTANDING AND STRENGTH

Persecuted? Facing enormous adversity? Then don't lash out. Don't reject the help God offers. Grasp His helping hand and fall to your knees in prayer. Thank God for the help that He is giving you and will continue to give you. Ask Him to send companions who can help. Ask Him for a supernatural strength to believe and to rejoice anyway!

Many of you know who Corrie Ten Boom was. Either you read the book or you saw the movie of her life, *The Hiding Place.*

Corrie Ten Boom participated in an underground railroad in the Netherlands during World War II. Untold numbers of Jews, who were hounded and hunted by the Gestapo, found escape in her house, where they were hidden in a remote, specially constructed room. Corrie, her sister Betsy, and her father hid numbers of Jews who are alive today, but would have been killed in concentration camps. But eventually the Gestapo caught up with the Ten Booms. They were sentenced to prison and hence to months of persecution.

I was so impressed with Corrie's story that I made a long-distance call to the Netherlands, which is where Corrie lived when I first met her. She came and spoke in our church. She was eighty years old at the time. I recently reread her unpublished sermon. It deserves a wider audience that I hope this book will offer. Here, then, is her testimony:

"Once I met a parachutist, and I asked him, 'When you jumped for the first time from an airplane to the earth, what did you think?'

"He said, 'I thought only one thing, and that was, "It works! It works!"'

"I am going to tell you that it works when you go with Jesus. Some people think that it does not work, and I hope that we will persuade them that they can never trust the Lord too much. The Lord said, 'In the world ye shall have tribulation: but be of good cheer; I have overcome the world' (John 16:33, KJV).

"Years ago my grandfather started a prayer meeting for the Jews. Every week he came together with his friends in an old watchmaker's shop. There he prayed for the peace of Jerusalem and the salvation of the Jews. That practice was so unusual that I remember the year when they started—1844. Today it is not unusual when Christians pray for the Jews.

"A hundred years later, in the very same house where my grandfather prayed for the Jews, his son—my father—four of my grandfather's grandchildren, and a great grandson were all arrested because they saved Jewish people in Holland during World War II. Four of them had to die in prisons. I came out alive. I cannot understand it, but that does not matter. We have to be ready for tribulation.

"I can tell you that I never had experienced such a realization of Jesus being with me as during the time when I was in the concentration camp. Ravensbruck, located north of Berlin in what is now East Germany, is far away from my home in Holland. The barracks where we lived, my sister Betsy and I, was in the shadow of a crematorium. Every day about six hundred bodies were burned there. When I saw smoke go up, I asked myself, 'When will it be my time to be killed?' I did not know beforehand that I should be set free by a miracle of God, and a blunder of man, one week before they killed all the women of my age.

"I have looked death in the eyes, not once but often. When you see death in people's eyes, you wake up to reality. What a joy it was that Jesus was with me, that I knew He had died on the cross for the sins of the whole world and also for my sins. I was not afraid. I knew that when they killed me I would go to the house of the Father with many mansions. I would go into the world of the living. What a joy! I knew the best was yet to be. How can we know how strong and rich we are in Jesus Christ and in His presence? By looking at the cross.

At the cross, at the cross
Where I first saw the light,
And the burden of my heart rolled away.
It was there, by faith, I received my sight.
And now I am happy all the day. *

"Sometimes in that terrible concentration camp we had to stand naked; they stripped us of all our clothes. Seven times I went through that ordeal. The first time was the worst; I could hardly bear it. I never felt so miserable, so cold, so humble. I said to Betsy, 'I cannot bear this.' Then suddenly, it was as if I saw Jesus at the cross. The Bible tells us they took His garments. He hung there naked. By my own suffering I could understand a fraction of the suffering of Jesus, and I was so thankful I could feel as He had felt. 'Love so amazing, so divine, demands my life, my soul, my all' [John Newton]. We must not forget we follow a scarred captain. Should we not have scars?

Under His faultless orders, we follow through the street.
Lest we forget, Lord, when we meet.
Show us your hands and feet.

"Jesus was with us, with Betsy and me, at the camp. In the morning we had to stand roll call very early. The chief of our barracks was so cruel that she sent us out a whole hour

*Isaac Watts.

234

early. Betsy and I did not go to the square where we would have to stand for hours during roll call; we walked around the tent. Everything was black. The ground was made black with coal. The barracks were painted black. The only light we had was from the stars and the moon. But Jesus was with us; He talked with us and He walked with us. Betsy said something, then He said something. How? I don't know, but we both understood what Jesus said. There was a little bit of heaven in the midst of hell.

"Once Betsy woke me in the middle of the night. 'Corrie, God has spoken to me. When we are set free we must do only one thing. We must bring the gospel over the whole world. We can tell so much experience, and that is why people will listen. We can tell them that here we have had real experience that Jesus' light is stronger than the deepest darkness. When we meet people who are in darkness, we can tell them that when they go with Jesus they cannot go too deep. Always deeper are His everlasting arms.' One week later, Betsy died. Two weeks later, I was set free.

"Christian, are you afraid of tribulation? Don't be afraid. Do you know that Paul once said, in 2 Thessalonians 1:4, 'We ourselves glory in you . . . for your patience and faith in all your persecutions and tribulations that ye endure: . . . Ye may be counted worthy of the kingdom of God, for which ye also suffer' (KJV)? Don't be afraid, for God did not give us a spirit of fear, but a spirit of love, and of power, coupled with a sound mind.

"I remember when I was a little girl. I once said to my father, 'Daddy, I am afraid that I will never be strong enough to be a martyr for Jesus.' Daddy replied, 'Corrie, when you plan to take a train trip, when do I give you the money for the train? Three weeks in advance?' 'No, Daddy, the day I leave.' Father then said, 'That is what God does. Today you do not need the power and the strength to suffer for Jesus, but the moment He gives you the honor of suffering for Him, He will also give you all the strength.' I was happy with his answer and went back to play with my dolls. In the books I have written, I have told how the Lord gave me the strength and all the grace when I was persecuted and suffered so terribly.

"Not long ago, when it was still possible but already dangerous to enter China, a missionary was asked, 'Are you not afraid?' She replied, 'I am afraid of one thing, that I shall become a grain of wheat not willing to die.' That is good. I hope that you will feel this way, too. I know the Lord has all the power and the strength available for you. Yes, also for you young Christians.

"Are you thinking that maybe it does not work when Jesus is with you? Do you know why you are thinking this? Because you have never tried working with Jesus. Try it. Give yourself to Jesus. Open your heart to Him. In His words, 'Behold, I stand at the door, and knock: if any man hear my voice, and open the door, I will come in' (Rev. 3:20, KJV).

"Did you hear His voice this morning? When will you

say, 'Yes, Lord, come in'? He will come in. He will not let you down. If you must go through dangerous and difficult times, don't be afraid, for Jesus is victor; Jesus is victor and Jesus will be victor forevermore. He is willing to make you and me more than conquerors!"

PASS TRIUMPHANTLY THROUGH THE PHASES

Now, to keep a positive, Be-Happy Attitude in painful times, remember: "This, too, shall pass away." Persecution is never eternal. To recover from persecution, be prepared to pass through three phases. The first phase is *collision*. This is the phase that occurs when the consciousness of the awful reality of the situation really hits you. Your peace suddenly clashes with conflict. This is the phase when you realize this horrible thing that is happening is not a dream. It's really happening—to you! The second phase is *withdrawal*. When you talk about fear, guilt, hatred, or anger, all of these emotions are expressions of the tendency to retreat, recoil, withdraw from accepting the horrible reality.

Collision is the first stage. Withdrawal is the second. Phase three is *adjustment*. In this third phase, you finally learn how to accommodate yourself to the loss. The only way you can reach this phase is to realize where you came from, who gave you what you have.

"The Lord gave . . ." Everything you have is from God.

Your very life is from God. But not as a gift—mind you. For life is not a gift from God; it is a sacred trust!

The story was in the papers—the tragedy of little David Rothenberg, who was set on fire by his troubled father. David suffered third-degree burns on much of his body, including his head and his face. He lost most of the fingers on his hands. But he is alive—and that is a miracle!

I count it an honor to have David and his remarkable mother, Marie, as dear friends. I know of no one who has faced more persecution than David. But when I met him I could see the sparkle in his eye. I could hear the humor in his voice. In spite of the physical deformities that David will have to live with all his life, as well as the emotional scars that he will always carry, he is a shining example of courage.

Of course, a great deal of credit goes to his mother. I shall never forget when she told me: "Dr. Schuller, it wasn't until the third day after the fire that I was able to turn Davy over to God. That's because those three days I was battling back and forth as to whether Davy should live or die. I didn't know if it was fair for him to live a life with such severe injuries. But when I gave it over to God and placed Davy in God's hands, then I knew I could accept God's will—whatever He decided would be best for Davy. Today, of course, I am very glad that David has lived. I feel that he's been a tremendous inspiration to millions of people throughout the country. He's been an example of courage, an example of faith. In fact he has given me more faith in God. Because of

Davy I know that God never gives us any more than we can handle."

Marie also shared with me how much it meant to David when her friend, Judy Curtis, read to David the parts in the New Testament that described the suffering of Jesus. David said to Judy, "They did that to Jesus—and He didn't do anything wrong!" David could relate to Jesus. And so he loves Jesus.

I was thrilled to be able to give David the Scars into Stars award that my church has given previously to Art Linkletter and Della Reese. It was the third time in the history of our ministry that I have given that award away. The award is a silver plate. For David we had inscribed on it these words:

"The Scars into Stars award presented to David Rothenberg in the Crystal Cathedral, Sunday, November 4, 1984, because you are turning your tragedy into a triumphant miracle by teaching millions of people the meaning of bravery in the face of incredible pain and suffering, the meaning of forgiveness in the face of unbelievable provocation, and how to turn a scar into a star by accepting Jesus Christ as Lord and Savior."

It is possible! No matter how great, how deep, how bitter the suffering—when we turn our trials over to Jesus, He can turn them into triumphs! He can do the impossible. He can work miracles. And He can carry us through the phases of collision and withdrawal into the healing phase of acceptance, if we but let Him.

I was first introduced to Rita Nightingale, a lovely young Englishwoman, through her book, *Freed for Life.** Her story is gripping. Compelling. And unbelievable.

Rita's story began in Bangkok, Thailand. She was ready to board her plane to Paris when she was suddenly called aside by an officer. She wasn't worried. She had nothing to hide—or so she thought. They took her to a room full of soldiers with machine guns and all kinds of weapons. They emptied all of her luggage. She still was not worried. Then they started to tear out the linings of the bag that her boyfriend had given her in Hong Kong, and they pulled out several small packets. They told her it was heroin.

From that moment on, no one told Rita anything. She was shocked and afraid because suddenly no one would speak English to her; everything that was said was uttered in a language foreign to her. The next thing she knew she was in a police cell.

Rita admits that she had been living a rather wild life, looking for adventure, yet she had never dreamed she would one day find herself in a prison cell. She had gone from being a glamour girl from Hong Kong to a cell in Thailand.

Glamour was one thing. Drugs were another. Rita had never been involved with hard drugs. The heroin was a shock to her. She had not put it there, so it must have been planted by someone.

Trying to convince the police in Thailand that she was

*Wheaton: Tyndale House, 1983.

innocent was an impossibility. The courts believed the police. She had been found with heroin in her possession, and that's all they cared about.

Rita was sentenced to twenty years in prison. The prison conditions were primitive—thirty women to a cell nine feet by fifteen feet. They slept feet to feet on the wooden floor with the mice and the cockroaches. You can imagine the rage and the bitterness Rita began to feel when it dawned on her what had actually happened. She had been used by a boyfriend who she had thought cared about her. The prospect that she would lose the next twenty years of her life was real. Her rage soon spread toward the whole world, even to the lawyers and embassy officials who were trying to help her.

When a lady came to visit her in prison and told her that God loved her, Rita was furious.

"How could God let this happen to me if He is so loving! If He loved me, I wouldn't be here!"

Then Rita had another visitor. She was an old lady—in her seventies—from Rita's hometown. Rita couldn't believe that this sweet little old lady would come all the way from England to Bangkok to talk to her.

When Rita heard her Lancashire accent, she started to cry. This was something for Rita, who had grown hard in the past months.

After the lady left, Rita asked herself over and over again, "Why?"

The little old lady had left a book with her. It was called, *The Reason Why*. In it Rita read the words of Jesus again. Although she had heard the story of Jesus before, it had never meant much to her in a personal way before. Through reading the book, she thought again about all she had wanted before—the excitement, the night life, the casinos. She had it all, but there was still something missing.

It took prison for God to open Rita Nightingale's eyes. She suddenly knew that Jesus was who He claimed to be, so she asked Him into her life.

Overwhelmed by the flood of emotions that came when she gave her life to Christ, Rita fled to the one and only private place in the prison—under the hospital hut. The buildings were all built on stilts, but no one ever went under them because of the snakes. It was there, under the hut with the snakes, that Rita's eyes were opened to the reality of eternal life. There, huddled in the darkness under the floor, she prayed and accepted Jesus Christ as her personal friend— her Lord, her God, her Savior.

It wasn't long before Rita noticed that her attitude was completely different. God didn't change the circumstances around her for a long time, but He began to change Rita and her attitude toward them.

Suddenly, one day, she was notified that she had been granted a pardon. No reason was given; the pardon came out of the blue. Rita attributes it to the fact that Christians around the world were praying for her.

She heard about her pardon through the news. That made it official. The news also said that the situation was very unique. Never before had a convicted drug smuggler been granted a royal pardon by the king of Thailand.

The day after Rita received the news of her pardon, the gates were opened and she was free. Today, Rita is a beautiful, born-again Christian. She is working in England for Chuck Colson in his prison ministries.

THE BEATITUDES— THE BE-HAPPY ATTITUDES

They were taught by one Man.

They were lived out by one Man. He remains himself the best example of how to deal with persecution.

He lived through persecution. He died by persecution. He rose again after the persecution. If you want to find happiness—real, deep, forever happiness—then wrap up your lessons on the Be-Happy Attitudes by learning more about this man who wrote them and lived them: Jesus Christ. I have referred to him as *the greatest possibility thinker who ever lived.*

Jesus should have been the world's greatest impossibility thinker. He had *nothing* going for Him.

Jesus was a member of a despised minority, a citizen of an occupied country, a nobody as far as the Romans were concerned, a joke to the occupying power, a nuisance to His fellow Jews.

God
will
have
the
last word
and
it
will be . . .
good!

Jesus lived among an oppressed, cynical, and embittered people!

Taxes were oppressive.

Freedom was unknown.

Survival was uncertain.

Religion was restrictive, negative, and joyless.

Yet, Jesus never made a politically inflammatory speech, never organized a guerrilla force, and never led a march on Jerusalem or Rome.

Jesus was from Nazareth, a city reputed to be culturally deprived and morally corrupt. "Can anything good come out of Nazareth?" was a common expression.

Jesus was not highly educated. Whatever His schooling was, it was simple. The only account of His writing was a note He scribbled in the sand.

Jesus had no organization. His followers were men with broken speech, rough hands, and cracked fingernails. They were unpolished, uncultured, unlettered, ignorant failures. In many ways, and in critical times, they proved to be unstable, uncertain, undependable, and disappointing.

Yes, Jesus knew ingratitude, rejection, misunderstanding, and betrayal.

By all the psychological laws of human development, Jesus should have died a judgmental, frustrated, critical, angry, unbelieving, cynical, rebellious, violence-prone, emotionally deprived, radically militant revolutionary!

Jesus remained unmarried, a single adult all His life. So

He spent His years without the encouragement, comfort, or companionship of a wife or children. In a society where children were a man's greatest treasure, He died never having fathered a single son or daughter.

Think of His death.

Jesus was only thirty-three years old! He was so young. He died before His mother! He was not given even a half-century, or more, to make His mark, write His books, build His empire, and conquer the world.

This—at least and at last—should have made Him a cynical impossibility thinker, crying out through tight lips, and bitter tears:

"It isn't fair!"

"I'm too young to die!"

"Oh God—give me more time!"

Jesus—where was His Heavenly Father when Jesus needed Him most?

Jesus—all His life He was good, kind, loving, and very religious. Every Sabbath He was in the synagogue. The Holy Scriptures—how He loved to read them. Prayer? His life was a prayer for all seasons!

Jesus.

How He loved His Heavenly Father.

How He trusted His Heavenly Father.

How He served His Heavenly Father.

Jesus. When He was on the cross, when He needed His God most—God seemed to have abandoned Him.

Jesus was persecuted—He was whipped, He was scorned, He was rejected, He was crucified—yet Jesus never once showed bitterness…. When He was on the cross He said, "Forgive them, for they know not what they do."

To Jesus every problem was a possibility in disguise.

Sickness was an opportunity for healing.

Sin was an opportunity for forgiveness.

Sorrow was an opportunity for compassion.

Personal abuse was an opportunity to leave a good impression and show the world how possibility thinkers react!

To Jesus every person was a gold mine of undiscovered, hidden possibilities!

Peter? A tough-talking fisherman. But—he could make a great leader of a great new church.

Mary Magdalene? A common prostitute. But—she could become a sensitive, sweet soul. She could one day anoint His body for burial.

Matthew? A vulgar materialist. But—he had possibilities to become a great writer! Even write a gospel!

To Jesus the important fact about you and me is not that we are sinners, but that we can be saints. So Jesus proclaimed the greatest possibility: The immeasurable MERCY of GOD.

To Jesus the whole world was jammed, pregnant, loaded, bulging with untapped, undiscovered, undetected POSSIBILITIES! Jesus really believed in the supreme possibilities!

Man *can* be born again!

Character *can* be changed!

You *can* become a new person!

Life *can* be beautiful!

There *is* a solution to every problem!

There *is* a light behind every shadow!

Yes! Jesus had an unshakable faith in these ultimate possibilities:

God exists!

Life goes on beyond death!

Heaven is for real!

Jesus was prepared to prove it. By dying—and rising again!

Jesus was impressed by what the world could become—never depressed by what the world was.

He truly believed that common people can become uncommonly powerful. He knew without a shadow of a doubt that ordinary persons could become extraordinary persons if they could become possibility thinkers.

So, Jesus made it His aim to give self-confidence to inferiority-complexed people. He made it possible for guilt-infected, failure-plagued, problem-swamped persons to start loving themselves and stop hating themselves!

He also gave hope to the hopeless, comfort to the comfortless, mercy to those whose hearts and lives were breaking all around them. He gave them the gift of abundant life and the secret of happy living through the Beatitudes:

"Blessed are the poor in spirit, for theirs is the kingdom of heaven."

"Blessed are those who mourn, for they shall be comforted."

"Blessed are the meek, for they shall inherit the earth."

"Blessed are those who hunger and thirst for righteousness, for they shall be satisfied."

"Blessed are the merciful, for they shall obtain mercy."

"Blessed are the pure in heart, for they shall see God."

"Blessed are the peacemakers, for they shall be called children of God."

"Blessed are those who are persecuted for righteousness' sake, for theirs is the kingdom of heaven. Blessed are you when men revile you and persecute you and say all kinds of evil against you falsely on my account. Rejoice and be glad, for your reward is great in heaven."

When Jesus spoke those words, was He thinking about His own persecution that lay ahead? Oh, yes, for surely no one has endured more persecution than Jesus. Surely we follow a scarred captain. He leads us nowhere that He has not walked Himself.

Jesus endured the physical persecution of the whippings, the crown of thorns, the nails in the hands and feet.

He died by one of the most painful of deaths—crucifixion. He also endured emotional persecution: He was taunted by the Romans who put a mock robe around His thrashed shoulders; a sign jeered down at him from the top of the cross—"The King of the Jews." When He asked for something to drink, they ridiculed Him even more by proffering up to him a sponge dipped in vinegar, and then laughed at His gasps and sputterings.

All the while, He endured the persecution of loneliness. He walked His "lonesome valley" all by Himself. The night before His arrest, Jesus prayed in the Garden of Gethsemane. None of His disciples, not even one out of twelve, stayed awake to pray with Him and comfort Him in His time of direst need. And when He was arrested, betrayed by the kiss of Judas, whom He loved and accepted into His inner circle of closest friends, the other disciples fled and even denied that they ever knew Him.

Jesus was arrested, placed on trial, and accused of blasphemy. Did He not claim to be the promised Messiah? At least, did He not allow people to get the impression that He was the Son of God? In His public trial He was challenged to deny His deity, to withdraw His blasphemous statements, and clear up the confused minds of the simple people who believed Him to be God visiting earth in human form.

But He could not tell a lie, so He remained silent. The verdict was predictable: death by crucifixion! A crowd gathered to see how a possibility thinker dies. How did He die? He died seeing and seizing the possibilities of the moment! He practiced what He had preached all His life! He turned His hell into a heaven. For here was His chance to save the soul of a lost thief who was being crucified beside Him.

This was a spectacular opportunity to dramatically teach all men and women of all ages to come that death can be a grand reunion with God! That scars can become stars!

Today the cross is the positive symbol of the happiest religion in the whole world. Persecuted? You and I can choose to be happy—anyway! For we believe that Jesus was resurrected on Easter morning! My personal conviction is this: Jesus Christ is alive this very moment!

What does Christ's persecution, crucifixion, and resurrection mean to us? It means that if we allow Christ to live in us, then it will be possible for us, also, to:

- Turn our problems into opportunities.

- Tackle our opportunities and succeed!

- Dream great dreams and make them come true!

- Switch from jealousy and self-pity to really caring about others who are much worse off than you are.

- Pick up the broken hopes and start over again!

- See great possibilities in those unattractive people!

- Become a truly beautiful person—like Jesus!

Now that you've studied all eight of the Be-Happy Attitudes, let me ask you a final question: *Are you really happy?*

Happiness—that deep inner strength that is made up of

courage, faith, hope, and peace. Mix them together, and you have happiness!

Happiness—the courage to hang on in the face of severe adversity!

Happiness—the faith that God will have the last word, and it will be good!

Happiness—the hope that, even though you can only see the shadow, someday the clouds will clear away and the sun will shine again!

Happiness—the quiet sense of self-esteem that comes when you know you have done your best.

Happiness—the assurance that you have been merciful and kind to enemy and friend alike.

Happiness—the quiet assurance that God will be merciful and kind to you, too.

Happiness—the beautiful belief that this life, no matter how difficult it may be, is not your final destination.

Your life here on earth is only a pilgrimage. Heaven—life with Jesus forever—is our eternal destiny.

> *I'm going to be happy today!*
> *Though the skies are cloudy and gray.*
> *No matter what comes my way—*
> *I'm going to be happy today!* *

In Christianity, we talk about "making a commitment" to

---

*Ella Wheeler Wilcox.

Jesus Christ. When we make that commitment, we raise the sail of faith. We sail and make this voyage in our little vessel across the turbulent ocean of life. But remember this: No sail has ever moved a ship. *The wind moves the ship.* The sail only catches the wind.

I'm asking you now to raise the sail of faith, and you will capture and harness the power of the spirit of God. Now that you have raised that sail of faith, keep it up there, even when you're in the spiritual doldrums. In God's good time the breeze will come. New positive feelings will replace the drab, old, boring, depressing, negative emotions. Fresh enthusiasm for life will come like a brisk breeze surging through you. You will experience a rebirth of youthful joy, energy, and excitement.

Here's how to make all this happen; pray this simple prayer: "Jesus, I need a friend as I journey through life. Right now I'm asking You to be my best friend and to keep the Be-Happy Attitudes flowing through my mind. Amen."

May
our beautiful Lord
give you
an
unexpected surprise
of joy
before every sunset
of your life!